T0350962

SIMPLE THINGS

SIMPLE THINGS
Lessons from the Family Farm

Jerry Apps

WISCONSIN HISTORICAL SOCIETY PRESS

Published by the Wisconsin Historical Society Press
Publishers since 1855

The Wisconsin Historical Society helps people connect to the past by collecting, preserving, and sharing stories. Founded in 1846, the Society is one of the nation's finest historical institutions.
Join the Wisconsin Historical Society: wisconsinhistory.org/membership

© 2018 by Jerold W. Apps

For permission to reuse material from *Simple Things: Lessons from the Family Farm* (ISBN 978-0-87020-887-4; e-book ISBN 978-0-87020-888-1), please access www.copyright.com or contact the Copyright Clearance Center, Inc. (CCC), 222 Rosewood Drive, Danvers, MA 01923, 978-750-8400. CCC is a not-for-profit organization that provides licenses and registration for a variety of users.

Printed in Canada
Cover linoleum print by John Zimm © 2018
Designed by Ryan Scheife, Mayfly Design

22 21 20 19 18   1 2 3 4 5

Library of Congress Cataloging-in-Publication Data
Names: Apps, Jerold W., 1934– author.
Title: Simple things : lessons from the family farm / Jerry Apps.
Description: Madison, WI : Wisconsin Historical Society Press, [2018] | Identifiers:
   LCCN 2018007673 (print) | LCCN 2018016260 (ebook) | ISBN 9780870208881 |
   ISBN 9780870208874 (hardcover : alk. paper) | ISBN 9780870208881 (ebook)
Subjects: LCSH: Farm life—Wisconsin—Anecdotes. | Family Farms—Wisconsin—
   Anecdotes. | Apps, Jerold W., 1934–
Classification: LCC S521.5.W6 (ebook) | LCC S521.5.W6 A668 2018 (print) | DDC
   630.9775—dc23
LC record available at https://lccn.loc.gov/2018007673

∞ The paper used in this publication meets the minimum requirements of the American National Standard for Information Sciences—Permanence of Paper for Printed Library Materials, ANSI Z39.48-1992.

It has long been an axiom of mine that the little things are infinitely the most important.

ARTHUR CONAN DOYLE

Contents

For my parents, Herman and Eleanor Apps, who taught me the importance of the simple things in life

Introduction

As I was walking around my farm the other day, I came upon an old cedar fence post. It was gray and weathered, with a decided lean to the east and a few pieces of rusty barbwire still attached. It was probably set in the ground by Weston Coombes, who farmed this property with his mother, Ina, until the early 1960s. The sight of that old fence post instantly took me back to my boyhood and days spent "making fence." When I was a kid on the home farm, it seemed we were always making fence, which meant digging holes with a posthole digger, setting new posts in the ground, and replacing barbwire where it had broken or rusted to the point that it was no longer useful.

Making fence was hard but necessary work, especially if you wanted to stay on the good side of your neighbors whose fields adjoined yours. No one wanted to get a call early on a Sunday morning (or any other day, for that matter) reporting that their cows had broken out and were in the neighbor's cornfield.

I didn't realize until years later that those hours spent making fence taught me many lessons—lessons that went far beyond basic fence repair. First, keeping your fences in good order shows respect for your neighbors and their hard work. They have enough challenges of their own without having to worry about your animals destroying their crops. Making fence also taught me the importance of doing things right: setting the posts properly so they stay in place, attaching the barbwires at appropriate distances apart so a cow can't step over or crawl under the fence, making sure everything is straight so that it "looks nice," as Pa used to say.

Today, as I dig through my shed and find old tools and other things left behind by the previous owner—pieces of horse harness, an old pulley from the hayfork that had been in the barn, and yes, a small roll of barbwire—I'm flooded with memories. Thinking about any one of these items, holding it in my hands and turning it to catch the light, I recall not just the role such tools and materials played in our everyday lives on the farm but also the many lessons I learned in using them.

On these pages, I write about what I learned from using a pitchfork and a shovel, a handsaw and a pair of pliers; what I learned from the animals that surrounded us and from the neighbors in our community. I recall the importance of the local train depot and the Mercantile in town, the Sears, Roebuck catalog and the radio programs we heard on our Philco broadcast from faraway cities like Milwaukee and Chicago. Almost always, I was learning without realizing it. And I surely was not aware that I was learning values that would stay with me my entire life and that went well beyond the borders of the family farm.

Nostalgia is a powerful emotion, especially for people in the autumn years of their lives. I know this firsthand, as I have shared my stories of growing up on the farm with hundreds of seniors over the past forty years. And as I share my stories, those listening recall their stories. Helping people remember their stories, as satisfying as that can be, is just the beginning of a process of reflection that can take us deeper, into an exploration of what we learned from our experiences—and of why our past matters. Our early histories largely determine the people we will turn out to be: what interests us, how we interact with others, how we contribute to the larger world, and what we value most in our lives.

I believe that those of us who grew up on farms, especially during the postwar years when agriculture was going through one of its great revolutions, learned much more than farm skills. We learned important lessons and values that are still with us today. During my talks, I often ask, "What of yesterday is worth keeping? What should be left behind?" Thinking about the lessons we glean from the deceptively "simple" things in life helps each of us answer that question for ourselves.

Fork, Hoe, Shovel, and Ax

If you grew up on a farm, you learned many skills. I learned how to pound a nail in a board without bending the nail or hitting my thumb. I learned how to tell the difference between a pine board and an oak board. (I learned that one the hard way. When Pa told me to find a board and fix the broken one in the calf pen, I grabbed the first board I could find from the pile in the shed and discovered, when I tried to pound a nail in it, that it was an old dried oak board that would not accept a nail, no matter how skilled I was with a hammer.)

I learned how to make a straight mark on a board with a metal carpenter's square and then to saw on the mark without wandering away from it. I listened to Pa's advice to "measure twice and saw once." As it turned out, that is good advice for living one's life—to think before acting, especially before speaking.

In addition to learning the proper way to use a hammer and handsaw, it was essential that I learn to use several other common farms tools. High on the list was a three-tine fork, used for making hay, pitching oat bundles, forking hay from the haymow in winter, and feeding hay to the cattle and horses. Starting at around age twelve, I had my own three-tine fork, just as my dad did. I also learned to use the larger six-tine fork, handy for handling manure, carrying straw from the straw stack to the barn, and digging potatoes and other root crops. Of course, weeds were a menace to our row crops, and we each had our favorite among the many hoes on the farm. We spent many a day hoeing everything from twenty acres of potatoes to an acre of cucumbers, a half-acre of strawberries, and the weeds in Ma's garden.

And then there were the shovels: from the gravel shovel, great for digging holes, digging around a pesky stone to remove it from a field, and any other digging that was required, to the scoop shovel, the best choice for moving grain and shoveling snow.

All of these tools—fork, hoe, and shovel—had wooden handles, and all required skills that allowed me to do the work quickly and well while not breaking the handle. Prying too hard might lead to a broken handle—and an unpleasant encounter with Pa, who would remind me once more how to properly use the tool.

Much of the work done with these tools was repetitive. Learning the rhythm of the work was essential, so I could do the work well and consistently while not having to do much thinking about what I was doing. As strange as it might sound, I learned to become one with the hoe, with the shovel, with the fork. The implement became an extension of me.

Using an ax properly is a specialized skill all its own. A well-sharpened ax is a dangerous tool, and Pa instructed my brothers and me carefully in its use. We had two kinds: a double-bitted ax, with two cutting edges, and single-bitted ax, with one edge for cutting and the other for pounding. We used both for making wood, which we did each fall and winter. To cut down an oak tree designated for firewood, we used the double-bitted ax to cut a notch about four inches high and as many wide into the trunk. Then we used a two-person crosscut saw to cut through the trunk, starting on the side opposite of the notch and cutting toward the notch. When the crosscut was aligned properly with the notch, the tree would fall toward the notch. When the tree was down, we sliced off the small branches with our axes, being exceedingly carefully to cut away from ourselves and to stay aware of the location of those working nearby.

Using a two-person crosscut saw takes a considerable amount of skill, as you have to pay attention to what you are doing at your end and to what the person on the other end is doing. The job, Pa stressed again and again, was to "let the saw do the work—don't force it." That meant: don't push the saw into the wood; let the saw's teeth do that on their own. And never push on the saw, only pull. If each person pulls on the saw, the process works well. But if one insists on both pushing and pulling, the saw is likely to jam, and all sawing ceases.

Using a crosscut saw taught me to be one both with the saw and with the person at the other end of the saw. This lesson has served me well over the years, as I have worked on many projects with one or more partners. When working cooperatively with one or more people, pull your share of the workload and avoid pushing, for pushing is sure to lead to trouble.

We used a single-bitted ax to split blocks of firewood into smaller pieces that would fit into our kitchen cookstove. Freshly sawed wood tended to split easier than wood that had been sitting in a pile for several weeks. Splitting oak wood was one of those higher-level skills that took several seasons to master. So much could go wrong. You could break the ax handle by chopping over the block (which meant you misjudged your swing, and the ax bit missed the block—but the handle didn't). You could bury the ax blade in the wood and find it nearly impossible to remove. Worst of all, you could strike the block with a glancing blow, and the ax could cut your leg or foot.

Pa taught me the importance of "reading" the wood. This means spending time examining the block of wood before you even pick up an ax—looking for knots that will make splitting difficult and observing the direction of the wood grain. With this knowledge, you can proceed with splitting. It takes time and practice to develop the skill of striking the block precisely in the spot your mind tells you is best, based on your reading of the wood. Once you've developed the necessary eye–hand coordination to aim and strike with precision, the work proceeds much more easily.

As I learned to use the basic tools necessary for work on the farm, I absorbed a good many other lessons that I wasn't aware I was learning, such as patience for repetitive tasks, respect for dangerous tools, and the value of working cooperatively to get the job done. Over the years, as I've worked with many people in a variety of settings, I've found that spending a little time reading the situation and the people involved can prevent wasted time and serious mistakes.

Pocket Tools

From my father I learned to carry two simple tools in my pocket at all times. Pa always carried a pair of pliers and a jackknife with him, except when he went to church. He said there was likely no call for either pliers or a jackknife in church, although he suggested some other tool might come in handy on those Sundays when the preacher went on and on with no stop in sight.

Pa carried the pliers in a little pocket on the side of his everyday bib overalls. The jackknife he toted in a front pocket. Scarcely a day passed that Pa didn't find a use for one or both of these basic but handy tools. It seemed a fence wire was always breaking; with a twist, the pliers could fix it. When a bolt had loosened, it was easily repaired with the pliers. When a nail needed a little hammering, once more the pliers appeared. And at the end of a hot day, when it was time for a cold beer from the icebox, the pliers snapped off the cap.

The jackknife had two blades, one larger than the other. The smaller blade was the sharper of the two, brought into action when a pencil needed sharpening, a rope must be cut, a sliver needed removing from a finger, or some whittling was necessary, as when fashioning a new stopper for the water jug. The larger blade came into play as a substitute screwdriver, to scrape dirt and grime from a farm implement, to slit open a letter, or to pry a board loose from a wooden crate.

"You never want to leave the house without a pair of pliers and a jackknife," Pa regularly reminded me.

Ma's favorite tool (though she would never call it that) was her apron. She always wore one, except when going to town or church. She sewed her aprons from flour sack cloth, fashioning long ones that covered most of her dress, from just below her chin down to her knees. Her favored aprons were those that had a cloth strap that fit over her head and tie strings in the back. She found uses for the apron that went well beyond protecting her clothes from splashes and spills. She used one apron corner to twist the cap off a jar of canned goods. She used the apron as a hot pad when grabbing a poker from the top of the woodstove. She used it to dry her hands and to wipe a bit of perspiration from her forehead as she cooked over the stove on a hot summer day. On occasion she used her apron to signal Pa in a far-off pasture, telling him to come home. Whenever one of my brothers or I scraped a knee or got kicked by a horse, Ma's apron was at the ready to dry our tears.

Just as Pa would never be caught without his pliers and jackknife, Ma was never without her apron when she was at home. And she always knew the whereabouts of a paring knife, her tool of choice for many tasks. She used the little short-bladed knife for everything from cutting the string on a well-wrapped package to paring an apple or a pan full of potatoes. The paring knife also came in handy for sharpening a pencil.

With their most reliable tools always at the ready, Ma and Pa taught me the importance of being prepared. Being able to fix something quickly, on the spot, saved time. If Pa spotted a broken fence wire while he was out cultivating corn, he could immediately repair it and not have to return later to do the fixing.

I also learned that the most essential items are those that can be used for multiple purposes. Ma's apron and paring knife proved themselves useful for myriad tasks—making them models of utility and efficiency that I've never forgotten.

Stove and Teakettle

Our farmhouse was built around 1900. Pa didn't know the exact year—he said it might have been a year earlier, the year he was born. He also said it didn't matter what year the house was built, but that it would last a long time if we took care of it, painted it once in a while, and kept the roof in good repair. It was a big house, with two bedrooms downstairs and three upstairs, plus a big kitchen, a dining room, and a parlor. My brothers and I were not allowed in the parlor. Ma kept that room neat and tidy—her words—so that the city relatives would be appropriately impressed and so the ladies aid women wouldn't find anything to complain about during their visits.

To look at the house, you couldn't help but be impressed by its size and its prominent place on the top of a little rise above the country road. The house appeared homey and inviting. But looks can be deceiving. Only two rooms in the house were heated: the kitchen, which had a wood-burning cookstove, and the dining room, which was heated with a Round Oak wood-burning heater. In winter, the other rooms in the house were as cold as a block of ice.

As a boy I learned that if we wanted to be comfortable during the cold months of the year, our woodstoves required constant attention. I also learned to recognize different kinds of wood and the amount of heat you could expect from each kind. Small pieces of pine make excellent kindling for starting a fire, but pine burns quickly, and, as Pa always said, it doesn't hold the heat. That's where oak wood excels. Getting it going takes some doing, but once oak begins burning, it generates a lot of heat and holds it for extended periods.

Like many farmers, Pa was deathly afraid of fire. He knew that if the house ever caught fire it would burn to the ground, as there were no firetrucks that drove into the country. With our reliance on wood-burning stoves and kerosene lamps with open flames, he had good cause to worry. If a lighted lamp tipped onto the floor or a stovepipe somehow became dislodged, a fire could result. If improperly dried wood was burned in the stove, a chimney fire could occur, leading to a house fire.

Sometimes I would wake up in the night in the cold second-story bedroom I shared with my twin brothers, hear crackling sounds, and wonder if a fire had started. I tried to smell smoke. It was easy to detect a bit of smoke smell when a house was heated with woodstoves, but was the smell more intense than usual? The following morning, when I would report to Pa that I had heard a crackling sound in the house walls, he would smile and say that it was probably a mouse or a rat crawling in the walls. (Rats and mice in the house were a constant problem, especially in the fall and winter.) Upon hearing my report, he would set another rattrap or two in the cellar to see if he could solve the problem, but he never did.

Often on a cold, dark night, with the wind rattling the windows, a strong gust would send a puff of smoke down the chimney of the big Round Oak stove and into the cozy dining room. Pa would say, "Storm coming"—and he was usually right in his predication. Even on such nights, my brothers and I were comfortable as we sat around the dining room table, doing our homework by the light of a kerosene lamp. Yet as cozy as the dining room was in the early evening, it was miserably cold the following morning, as fire in the old woodstove went out about midnight. The kitchen cookstove fire would also die in the night, and the entire house was colder than the inside of an icehouse come morning until Pa got the fire going again.

My mother cooked and baked in the wood-burning cookstove. She gauged the oven heat by opening the oven door and putting her hand inside, which told her when to add another piece of oak wood to maintain the temperature she wanted. She tried to teach her boys that skill, but I didn't get past learning the heating qualities of various types of wood. I did, however, learn that a wood-burning stove could produce delicious homemade bread, apple pie, chocolate cake, sugar cookies, and sweet rolls. Today I cook on a wood-burning cookstove at my farm, always trying to remember what my mother taught me about its use.

Although we always appreciated our wood-burning stoves for their ability to warm us on the coldest mornings, we took for granted the old and dented teakettle that sat at the back of the kitchen stove. Made of aluminum dulled by age, the kettle held about four quarts of water. From early morning until long after we crawled up the frigid stairway to our beds, a thread of steam poured from its spout. I remember only once or twice—when a persnickety city relative appeared and insisted on having tea—that the teakettle was used for that purpose. With no indoor plumbing, the teakettle was our only source of hot water.

Hot water was especially important when winter illnesses came our way. Mixed with salt, it soothed a sore throat. A glass of hot water mixed with a jigger of "medicinal" whiskey became a whiskey sling that would kill most any cold. For bruises, sprains, and aches of assorted origin, Ma filled the rubber hot water bottle with hot water from the teakettle. She wrapped a towel around it, and the hot water bottle became a warm friend on a cold winter night.

We might even use hot water from the teakettle to thaw a frozen water pump, de-ice a slippery step, or thaw a frozen pig trough. That teakettle, the humblest of objects, improved our lives in untold ways.

Porch

One of the most important places in our farmhouse was not inside the house at all. On hot summer evenings, when the chores were done, our whole family gathered on the back porch to rest, reflect on the day, and make plans for the day to come.

I remember one summer evening when I was about ten years old. The western sky was a collage of reds, pinks, and purples as the late-June sun slipped below the horizon and the coolness of evening began settling over the land. Fingers of mist rose from the valleys, and the last robin sang its evening song. In the distance I heard a cowbell, a signal that the neighbor's cows were grazing in their night pasture on the long hillside that we could still see from our farmyard as the evening light slowly gave way to darkness.

We had gathered on the porch after the evening milking. We talked about the day, about the hay crop, about the corn and oats and how well they were growing, about the hay-mower that needed replacing one of these years.

It was nearly dark now; through the kitchen window I saw the dim light radiating from the kerosene lamp resting on the table, a quiet yellow beacon. Fireflies skittered here and there, specks of cold light that came on strong and then trailed off, like tiny flashlights with wings.

Pa shared a story about an earlier time when he was a lad and his family was making hay—wild hay, for his father hadn't known about alfalfa and red clover. Pa told about cutting the hay with horses, about raking it and piling it into bunches to dry and then hauling it into the cow barn with a steel-wheeled wagon and pitching it into the haymow. By hand. With a three-tine pitchfork. I thought about the fact that his story took place forty years earlier, and yet we still made hay in almost the same way, with horses, three-tine pitchforks, and a steel-wheeled wagon.

We sat quietly for a time, no one saying anything. Then we heard it, the whippoorwill in the field in back of the house, near the strawberry patch and not far from the woods. It repeated again and again: "Plant your corn, plant your corn." That's what Pa said the bird was calling. Ma said the bird cried, "Whip poor Will." We had a neighbor named Will, so the call felt personal—and inappropriate, because we liked Will. We counted the calls, five, ten, sometimes twenty in a row before the bird paused. In the distance we heard an answer, another whippoorwill calling, "Whip-poor-will, whip-poor-will." Were these messages of love? Probably, but we didn't talk about such things. We just listened to the night birds call to each other and to us.

Ma said that Uncle Charlie and Aunt Sophia were coming to the farm for a couple weeks of vacation in July. Pa remembered how Uncle Charlie always complained that the whippoorwill kept him awake at night. Pa didn't like Uncle Charlie; he said he complained about everything, and he was lazy. "You gotta put up a stick to see if he's moving," Pa said about Uncle Charlie.

From the freshly mowed hayfield in front of the house, we smelled the alfalfa and sweet clover drifting on the night air, tantalizing us with an aroma that has never been matched by the finest perfume makers in the world.

Pa dug his pocket watch from his bib overalls and held it up to catch a glimmer of light from the kitchen lamp. "About nine," he reported. "Time for bed. Sunup before you know it."

We all filed into the house and to bed. The smell of new-mown hay drifted through my open bedroom window, and I heard the whippoorwill calling again and again as I drifted off to sleep.

I remember so well those summer evenings on the back porch of our old farmhouse. The five of us enjoyed being together and the pause after our day's work to listen to a story or two from Pa and enjoy the sights, sounds, and smells of nightfall. Those times on the back porch taught me much about appreciating the things that money could not buy.

Chores and Work

Pa crawled out of bed in a freezing cold bedroom, as the two woodstoves heating the house had gone out around midnight. He lit the kerosene lamp that stood by his bedstead and pulled on a wool shirt, a pair of wool pants, and bib overalls. He walked into the dining room, where he started the fire in the big Round Oak heater, then to the kitchen, where he started the cookstove with pine kindling wood and a bit of kerosene. A pail filled with drinking water stood on a corner of the sink. Depending on how cold the outside temperature was, the drinking water might be topped with a quarter-inch or more of ice. Pa placed the water pail on the stove so the ice would thaw and my mother would have water to make coffee when she got up a half-hour or so later.

Between starting the fires, Pa woke me up by rapping on the stovepipe leading to the frigid bedroom above the dining room. Then, with both stoves going, Pa pulled on his wool barn coat, heavy woolen cap, and six-buckle boots. He lit a barn lantern and headed for the pump house, where he started the fire that kept our pump from freezing. Then he walked the narrow path to the outside cattle tank, which was covered with ice. He started the wood-burning tank heater that would melt the ice so the cattle would have water when they were let out to drink later in the morning.

Next he walked the narrow, shoveled path through the snow to the potato cellar, a building built in the side of the hill just beyond the chicken house. Here is where we stored our fall crop of potatoes as we waited for the price to come up in late winter. A stove in the potato cellar kept the potatoes from freezing, and Pa started that one next.

It was only then that he was ready to begin the morning milking. By that time he expected that I would show up in the barn to help. Not once did I hear him complain about the cold or about all the fire-starting. It was winter, after all, and that is what you did when you lived on a farm in Waushara County in 1946. We had no electricity, and very little about our lives was "automated." These were chores that had to be done every day, 365 days of the year.

Pa made a distinction between chores and work. Chores were mostly the same, day after day, month after month— feed the cows and milk them twice a day; feed the calves, hogs, and chickens; carry in wood; carry water from the pump house to the kitchen. Chores were more difficult in winter, as we had to contend with freezing temperatures and belly-deep snow.

Work, on the other hand, was tied directly to the seasons and took up the time between doing chores on either end of the day. Work included planting and hoeing potatoes, making hay, harvesting grain, threshing, filling silo, shocking and husking corn, and making wood.

I learned much from the repetition of doing chores. Most chores, although seemingly boring and devoid of anything new, had to be done well and on time no matter what. There was no skipping a chore. If you were sick and couldn't do your chores, it was your responsibility to make sure one of your brothers did them for you, as you would do for your brother when he wasn't feeling well. If Pa was sick—which he seldom was—my two brothers and I did his chores.

Ma had her chores, too: fixing three meals a day, washing and mending our clothes, feeding the chickens and gathering the eggs, taking care of the garden from planting time in late April until the last vegetable was harvested in fall. If Ma was sick, Pa and my brothers and I pitched in to do her chores. But the cooking suffered. None of us, especially Pa, could cook as well as Ma.

Work could also be boring, but a particular work project usually lasted only a few days. Making hay generally began in early June and continued well into July. When Pa declared the hay crop ready for harvesting, he would hitch the team to the McCormick five-foot sickle-bar mower and head out to the hayfield. Fresh hay, clover, timothy, and alfalfa sometimes stood three feet tall. With the mower's passing, it toppled to the ground to dry in the sun.

If the day was warm, with bright sunshine and a southerly breeze, and the crop was not too tall and rank (that is, coarse and tangled), the hay would be ready for raking and bunching by late afternoon. With the hay sufficiently dry, Pa hitched the team to the high-wheeled dump rake with half-moon iron tines some four feet high. Compared to the sickle-bar mower, it pulled easily. The team walked briskly around the field, raking the loose, drying hay into long rows. While Pa drove the team, my brothers and I were stuck hoeing potatoes, beans, or cucumbers, or maybe helping Ma pick strawberries.

Bunching hay was not quite as boring as hoeing. It seemed we never finished hoeing. Bunching hay had a visible end, although several of our hayfields were twenty acres and the hay bunches seemed to go on forever. Starting at the end of a raked row, you would use your three-tine fork to push the hay into a round, neat pile—it had better be neat because if it tipped over, Pa would let you know about it—then top it off with a sizable forkful and move on to the next bunch. One bunch after the other until dozens of them lay behind you, dozens and dozens. You didn't want to see another one, ever.

You couldn't cheat when bunching hay. You either made a hay bunch, or you didn't. When you hoed you could slack off, move a little more slowly, even skip a weed or two—but you'd best not be caught doing it.

After Pa finished raking, he tied up the team and helped us. Pa made bunching hay look easy. He had a rhythmic, free-flowing, easy style, with no wasted effort. He could make two bunches for every one I made, and he seemed to enjoy every minute of the process. It took me a while to catch on, but many of the tasks had a rhythm to them, and once you learned the rhythm, you could do the task well and not have to give much thought to it. In other words, I could work and still think about such things as a cute neighbor girl, what I might be studying in school next fall, and the ice cream cone I was looking forward to enjoying on Saturday night when the family went to town.

When bunching hay, every bit of effort, or lack of effort, was visible. The best part—aside from that wonderful smell of drying clover, timothy, and alfalfa—was looking out over a finished field of hay bunches aligned from one end to the other. At day's end, my brothers, Pa, and I stood at the end of the field leaning on our forks. Pa didn't say much, except perhaps for a comment or two about how good or poor the hay crop was compared to last year. He didn't say it in so many words, but he wanted my brothers and me to appreciate not only the hard work that we had done but also the beauty of what we had created—the results of our labors stretching before us in long, straight rows. A field of sweet-smelling hay bunches was rural beauty at its finest.

Both chores and work were an integral part of farm life when I was growing up. Both were necessary, and neither could be avoided. Properly learned skills were involved, of course, and developing a rhythm made the work easier. But perhaps more important, I learned that every chore or work project—even a particularly detested one—had to be done, and done well. Pa never expected my brothers and me to do everything perfectly. What he said was, "Do the best you can with what you've got." He didn't issue a lot of praise or require perfection, but he did expect effort—trying hard to do well within one's physical and mental abilities. The best thing that a parent could hear said by a relative or neighbor was, "That kid is dependable."

My pa worked hard all his life, starting when he was pulled out of fifth grade because he was deemed big enough to work. He never complained about working. I believed he looked forward to it, no matter whether it was as complicated as running a threshing machine or as simple as hoeing the weeds from a row of potatoes. Almost all farmwork was outside, and I'm sure that was one of the reasons Pa never complained: he loved the out-of-doors. But above all, Pa valued work. Perhaps he developed that attitude during the Depression years, when he saw so many people without work and suffering mightily. Working at his side, I not only learned to do the chores and work associated with farming, I also developed a positive attitude toward work, no matter how menial or complicated or unpleasant the conditions.

Barn Lantern

On a cold winter morning, after dressing in front of the dining room wood burner, I pulled on my old Mackinaw winter coat, slipped on my wool cap with the fur ear laps, and retrieved my barn lantern from its place near the kitchen woodbox. I took a match from the matchbox on the wall near the kitchen stove, lifted the lantern's glass globe, struck the match, and touched the flame to the lantern's wick. Then, carrying my lantern by its heavy wire handle, I was on my way to the barn, where Pa had gone a few minutes earlier.

The lantern cast long shadows on the snowscape as I walked briskly along the narrow path we had shoveled through the snow. Upon arriving at the barn, I hung my lantern from a nail behind the cows. Pa's lantern already hung from a nail at the other end of the barn.

Grabbing my three-legged milk stool and a milk pail, I cozied up to a cow and began milking. Except for the sound of fresh milk zinging against the bottom of the milk pail and the occasional rattle of a cow's stanchion, it was quiet in the barn. The two lanterns provided just enough soft yellow light for us to see what we were doing.

When I finished milking my assigned cows, with lantern in hand I climbed the ladder on the west wall of the barn to the haymow above the stable, which housed the cows and our team of horses. My daily task was to throw down hay from the haymow and then toss the dried hay through the hay chutes that dropped it in front of the cows' stalls.

Arriving in the cold and frosty haymow, I hung my lantern on a nail pounded into one of the barn's wooden beams, well away from where I would be tossing hay and thus avoiding any chance of a fire. The warm, moist air from the cattle housed below filtered to the haymow and gathered on the huge cobwebs found there. The moist air froze on the cobwebs, making wonderful pieces of art—at least, that is how I thought of those beautiful cobweb creations. The soft, yellow light of the lantern made them even more beautiful.

By the early 1930s, most people who lived in cities and towns had central heating, indoor plumbing, and electricity. But lamps and lanterns still lit the rural countryside in central Wisconsin and many other rural locations. In 1936, President Franklin Roosevelt's Rural Electrification Act was passed by the US Congress, and REA co-ops began stringing lines in the country. However, shortages during World War II led to a halt of that project—leaving lines strung within a half mile of our farm. And so my family and many others in our community continued to use kerosene lamps and lanterns to light our way.

When electricity did finally arrive at our farm, in 1947, we could leave our lanterns behind and walk to the barn in the glare of an electric yard light. With the flip of a switch, the barn was as bright as a summer day. The trade-off was that now we had to pay a monthly electric bill, which amounted to several times more money than fifteen cents a gallon for kerosene that lasted a week, sometimes longer. And now we depended on someone else to provide for a basic need we were used to handling on our own. While my parents, like most other rural people, adjusted to the change, they taught me to keep my old standby barn lantern handy. When the power went out—and it did, sometimes during storms, sometimes for no apparent reason—I would still be able to find my way.

Old Barn, New Barn

Pa never liked the old barn that was on our farm when he began renting the place in 1924. It was too small and inconvenient, with limited space for hay storage and no mechanical hay fork. Forking loose hay from a hayrack into one of the two outside doors that led to the haymow was an absolutely miserable job. You'd drive the team with the hay wagon alongside one of these barn doors and then, with a long-handled three-tined pitchfork, push the hay through the open door. A second person forked the hay into the back corners of the little haymow until the barn was filled to the rafters.

The procedure worked fairly well unless the day was exceedingly hot, say, in the low 90s. But almost any farm job around the buildings was unpleasant when it was that hot. When the hayrack was full, pitching the hay through the open doors was easier, as the person pitching was closer to the door. As he worked his way from top to bottom, unloading the hay, the job became more difficult. That last few forks-full were the worst, as the fellow had to pitch the hay high over his head, with a cloud of hay leaves sifting down his sweaty neck. Pa hated it, but he was not one to complain. I hated it, and I did complain.

I knew Pa wanted a better barn, especially during the years when we never had enough hay storage space to last our herd of dairy cows through the long winters. On the south end of the old barn, Pa, with the help of several neighbors, constructed a rickety hay shed that was half as long as the barn, nearly as high, and had a roof but no sides. It was easier to fill the hay shed than the barn, but the rain and snow blew in on the hay, spoiling some of it. And it was an additional chore to carry the hay from the hay shed to the barn, where the cattle spent the winter.

In addition to the storage space in the barn and the hay shed, if the hay crop had been good—we usually grew about thirty acres of alfalfa mixed with red clover—we also constructed a haystack near the barn, sometimes more than one. Building a haystack took some skill to make sure that the sides remained straight as more and more hay was piled onto it and that the loose hay was evenly distributed on the stack as it grew taller. If a haystack tipped over, we would have to rebuild it. And if a neighbor drove by and saw the tipped stack, it would be the subject of an embarrassing story that would spread throughout the neighborhood. We all were on the lookout for such minor catastrophes.

Once the haystack was built, Pa covered the top with a roll of tarpaper, weighted down with additional loose hay. This helped to prevent weather damage, but only somewhat. And again, the hay from the haystack had to be carried into the barn, another tedious, difficult task. Pa wanted a bigger barn, one with a mechanical hayfork that would pull the hay from the hay wagon and drop it into the haymows. He could not afford to build a new barn; these were the early years of World War II, and farmers had not yet recovered from the Great Depression. But with milk prices somewhat higher by the mid-1940s, Pa could afford an addition to the present barn, so he looked for an existing barn to buy. In 1946, he found one for sale about four miles from the home farm. He paid $500 for the barn and another $350 to move it. With the help of a moving crew, he hauled it to the farm.

We took the old hay shed down. Now, with the new barn attached to the south end of the old barn, work was easier on the Apps farm, at least during haying season, as the new barn had a mechanical hayfork to move the hay from the hay wagon to the haymows. No more hay shed. No more haystacks.

Pa waited twenty years to get a better barn. He never lost sight of wanting one, but he also was dead-set against borrowing money. He didn't have a better barn until he could afford it and could pay with cash. From him I learned the value of having a goal to work for. And I learned the importance of waiting until you have enough money before buying something, no matter how much you might want it.

The Little Things

Those of us who grew up during the Depression and World War II had little in the way of material possessions, but we learned to appreciate what we did have. As a farm kid, I learned to appreciate a cool drink of well water on a hot day, the beauty of a sunset, the taste of fresh peas from our garden, and the sheer joy of hearing much-needed rain drumming on the barn roof.

On our Saturday night trips to town, Pa sometimes bought a half-gallon of ice cream. Neapolitan was our favorite, as we could enjoy three flavors—strawberry, chocolate, and vanilla—all in one. The fellow at the ice cream store wrapped the container in an old newspaper. Without electricity and thus relying on an icebox rather than a refrigerator, we had no way to store ice cream. So when we returned from town, usually around nine in the evening, Pa lit the kerosene lamp on the kitchen table and fetched his favorite butcher knife, the one that my grandfather Witt had made from a piece of steel that he had sharpened to a razor edge, with a wooden handle riveted to the blade. Ma took five plates from the cupboard while Pa unwrapped the newspaper from the ice cream container. With the long knife, Pa cut the half-gallon block of ice cream into five equal slices, placing a slice on each plate. Then, with every bit of ice cream gone, we all scampered off to bed, to be awakened at five thirty the next morning to begin another week of hard summer work.

During haying season in late June and July, it was a welcome surprise to drive our team of horses into the dooryard hauling an enormous load of loose hay and be greeted by Ma holding four bottles of homemade root beer. Pa bought Hires root beer extract from the Mercantile in Wild Rose, and he and Ma made up a batch each spring, bottling the tasty liquid in dark brown beer bottles and capped with a bottle capper—bottles and capper no doubt left over from Prohibition days. They kept the bottles of root beer cool in the cellar under our house. How wonderful it tasted on those hot days.

My brothers and I had few store-bought toys. We usually found one toy and one article of clothing under the tree on Christmas morning. On our birthdays we received gifts as well, but they were usually practical in nature: a shirt, a sweater, or the like, although when I turned twelve and thus old enough to have a hunting license, I received a very special gift, a new hunting knife. But one of my most hoped-for gifts was a new book. I have always been a great lover of books, and my parents and aunts and uncles knew this and sometimes gave me books as presents. I still have most of them on my bookshelf, including *Midnight* (a story about a wild horse) by Rutherford Montgomery, *Hans Brinker* (a story of life in Holland) by Mary Mapes Dodge, and *The Black Arrow* (historical fiction taking place in England) by Robert Louis Stevenson.

Receiving a new pair of bib overalls always felt like a special occasion. I usually got a new pair before school started in the fall and another before the annual Christmas program at our country school. I've never forgotten the smell and feel of new blue denim and how privileged I felt; many of my schoolmates' parents did not have enough money to buy new bib overalls for their children. One friend's mother made overalls out of denim cloth for her boys. Thankfully, even though I thought new store-bought bib overalls were far superior to handmade ones, I also learned well from Pa never to brag.

Cows

I learned a lot from a small herd of cows. We never had more than fifteen or twenty milk cows, and maybe ten young stock, which were heifers not yet milking. We pastured them from April until October, depending somewhat on the weather on both ends of the pasturing season and whether there was any pasture to eat. During the winter months, the cows stayed in the barn, locked into stanchions that fit around their necks, but we put them outside to exercise in the barnyard most winter days.

Each cow had its own stall in the barn, and each one headed to her designated spot, no matter what the weather or the time of year. Thus, we were always assured of finding the same cow in the same place. Each cow had a name: Florence, Sadie, Ethyl, Mabel, Doris, . . . Each had its own personality as well. Some of them enjoyed being milked. Those cows just looked around at me when I grabbed my three-legged milk stool and slid under them, grabbed two of their teats, and began squeezing fresh milk into the milk pail I held between my legs. Others hated being milked and let me know it by trying to put a hind foot into the milk pail or attempting to kick me or swat me in the face with a wet tail. Those belligerent cows we called kicker cows.

Josephine was an otherwise obedient and good-looking Holstein. She took her stall in the barn without encouragement, always ate her hay and silage, and never knew a sick day. At four years old, she gave lots of milk, filling a sixteen-quart pail twice a day. But she was a kicker cow. Pa didn't know if she was ticklish or simply had an ornery streak. About once a week—there was no predicting this event— it would happen. I would be milking one of my assigned cows, and Pa would be milking Josephine. All was quiet and content in the barn, the only sounds the occasional rattle of a stanchion. Then, with no warning, I would hear a *Ka-BANG!* and see Pa's milk pail sail out into the alley behind the cows, splashing milk all over the concrete floor. Pa's reaction was always the same. After he picked himself up from the straw-covered barn floor, he would announce, "I'm gonna sell that damn cow the first chance I get!" He spoke in a loud enough voice to startle the rest of the cows in the lineup.

Pa was always optimistic that Josephine would get over her problem. Some cows did, and Pa had enough patience to wait it out—to a point. However, Josephine seemed destined to continue her unpredictable mayhem, and the whole sequence (milking, *ka-BANG!*, spilled milk, Pa's pronouncement) kept playing out.

One day a cattle dealer stopped at the farm, as they did from time to time.

"Got any good cows for sale, Herman?" he asked.

"I do," Pa said. They were both leaning on the barnyard fence, looking at the cows. My twin brothers and I stood nearby.

"That big Holstein over there gives a lot of milk and eats well, but I'm running out of room in the barn, and I'm going to have to let her go," Pa said with nary a smile on his face.

"Good-lookin' cow," the dealer said.

"She is that," Pa said.

"What'll you take for her?" the dealer asked.

"Should be worth three hundred dollars," Pa said.

"Give you two and half," the dealer said.

"She's yours," Pa answered. The men walked into the house to settle up; my brothers and I stayed outside. Soon Darrel and Donald began to sing, "Pa sold the kicker cow, Pa sold the kicker cow."

On his way to his car, the dealer paused.

"What are those kids singing?"

"Oh, some little song. Those kids are always making up songs. You know how kids are," Pa quickly replied. Long after the dealer had driven away and the dust had settled again on the road past our farm, Pa had not yet finished telling my brothers that they'd almost lost a sale for him.

As I think back on Josephine, I know I learned several things from the situation. Patience is a good quality, but there are times when our patience is challenged and we have to make a decision. Cattle dealers in those days had a reputation for outwitting farmers and buying animals worth more than they were willing to pay. I was proud of Pa, who outwitted the cow dealer that day. (Though we could discuss whether not revealing the cow's major fault, his true reason for selling her, was ethical.) And my brothers learned, after a tongue-lashing from Pa, to stay silent when adults are talking business.

Generally, our cows got along with one another. The presence of a boss cow helped. She was always in the lead when the herd, in single file, walked from the pasture, down the dusty lane to the barn, twice a day. How the herd selected the boss cow remained a mystery. Perhaps she took the leadership responsibility on by herself, as she was usually an older cow that the others respected. Or maybe she earned the role in a head-butting contest with another cow for the boss role, something I observed a time or two.

The boss cow would stay in her role as leader for as long as she remained on the farm and was able to carry out her leadership duties—sometimes as long as ten years. Later in life, when I occasionally wondered if some group I was involved in didn't really need a leader, I remembered our boss cows, who in their quiet way kept the herd working together and got things done—even if the goal was as simple as returning home from the pasture in an orderly fashion.

When a calf was born on our farm, teaching it to drink from a pail was often my job. Drinking from a pail is a learned skill, as a calf's natural way of taking sustenance is directly from its mother, nuzzling her udder until it discovers a teat and then begins sucking. To teach a calf to drink from a pail, first you must corral the little calf (this is the easiest part of the process) and then straddle it between your legs, holding the hungry little animal firmly in place. Grab the pail half-filled with milk from the calf's mother, stick your hand into the warm milk, and encourage the calf to suck on your fingers. Once the calf begins to suck, gently push its muzzle into the pail of warm milk, hoping it will continue sucking when you remove your fingers from its mouth. At this point in the process, you learn that each little calf, like every cow, has its own personality. Some calves take immediately to drinking milk from a pail; others take three or four tries. Some little bovines seem to take pleasure in sticking their muzzle in the pail of milk and then tossing their head up and out of the pail, soaking your pants.

That last one happened frequently, and it taught me to control my temper and keep patience ever firmer in my grasp. I also learned that not all teaching is comfortable—think wet pants and a challenged ego (after all, I was bigger and smarter than this little creature)—and that some lessons must be taught many times before they set in. It turned out that newborn calves are not that much different from some of the students I would work with later on.

Stormy

In 1947, my 4-H dairy project was a little bull calf that I had named Stormy. That was the year I was recovering from the polio that had paralyzed my right knee from January to April. That summer I was relearning how to walk, a difficult and discouraging task. At the same time, I was teaching Stormy to lead in preparation for the county fair in August. It was no small task, and many days I simply wanted to give up. Working with a reluctant little calf added to my woes. Pa, ever the optimist, advised, "Be patient with Stormy. He has a mind of his own, but eventually he will learn how to lead." I wasn't sure it would happen. But that year I was eligible to stay overnight at the fairgrounds on Friday and Saturday nights of the fair, and I was determined to do it, balky bull calf or not.

It wasn't until years later that I realized that the little bull calf had really been my physical therapist. Pa's plan was to get me walking again, and by summer's end he had mostly succeeded. By fair time, when Stormy felt like it, he led well. When he didn't feel like it, which was often, he was a handful. He'd rather run away with me holding on to the lead strap and stumbling along behind him, or stand with all four feet planted, refusing to move at all. Neither of these behaviors was acceptable in the show ring and would likely result in me receiving a pink ribbon—or even being disqualified.

Opening day for the county fair arrived. Ross Caves, our livestock trucker, arrived to pick up Stormy and me, along with a couple bags of loose hay that I would feed Stormy while we were at the fair. When we arrived at the fairgrounds, located on the south side of Wautoma, I helped Caves load and unload calves. Then I was alone with Stormy in the cattle barn at the county fair—both of us more than a little anxious about what would happen the following morning when I led (or tried to lead) Stormy into the show ring where the cattle judge stood, looking carefully at each animal before lining us and giving out the ribbons: blue for first prize, red for second, white for third, and pink for fourth. Of course, every 4-H member wanted his or her calf to receive a blue ribbon, but we were also taught to not complain if we received a ribbon of a color other than blue.

Our 4-H club had raised enough money to purchase an army surplus tent, where some of my fellow 4-H'ers (boys only) would spend the night with our leader, Clayton Owens. While I waited for the others to arrive, I walked down the midway, lined on both sides with food tents, rides, and games of chance. I smelled hamburgers with onions; twenty-five cents, the sign read. But I knew I'd best not buy one, as Pa had said I should walk downtown and eat at the Wautoma Restaurant. By seven that evening, the other 4-H members had arrived and located their folding surplus army cots in our surplus army tent. And by nine, as it was getting dark, we all tried to sleep. The next day would be a big one as we prepared our calves for the show ring and then led them in front of the judge and a crowd of spectators.

I was up at five-thirty the next morning to feed, water, and provide fresh bedding for Stormy. Next I began preparing him for the show ring. I polished his horns with black shoe polish to make them even blacker. I washed the white switch hair at the end of the little bull's tail. I brushed him until there was nary a loose hair or a single piece of dust on his black and white coat. All the while I talked softly, telling him everything was going to be okay and that if he did what I asked him to do in the show ring, all would turn out well. Stormy seemed as nervous as I was. We were in a strange place with strange cattle nearby and strange people around us, some of them stopping and staring at us as I tried to brush away both our jitters.

Finally, the show ring announcer said, "The next class will be Holstein junior bull calves." That was us. I removed the manger halter and pulled the black leather show halter over Stormy's head, the one that Mr. Gorman, the harness maker in Wild Rose, had made for me. I backed Stormy into the walkway, and we headed for the show ring, moving people aside as we walked. Stormy walked with his head high, as I had taught him. But would he continue to do so when we entered the show ring and a critical cattle judge began eyeing both of us?

Stormy and I walked around the show ring, with another bull calf and boy pair ahead of us and another behind us. Once around the ring, slowly. Stormy was on his best behavior. He was doing better than he had ever done at home, considerably better. Then the judge motioned for me to pull my calf up to the side of the ring and stop. I was thrilled, for Pa had said the judge always picks out the blue ribbon winners first. Pa was right. Stormy received a blue ribbon.

I learned a great deal from showing cattle, which I would go on to do for ten years at the Waushara County Fair and the Wisconsin State Fair in Milwaukee. I learned not to gloat or brag when my calf received first prize and not to despair if he received fourth prize. When I came out on the bottom, Pa was never critical. He would simply say, "Next year you'll do better."

In addition to all that was involved in preparing an animal for the show ring, I learned the joys and surprises of developing a close relationship with an animal. We had our ups and downs, but I'm sure I learned as much from Stormy as he learned from me.

Frank, Charlie, and Dick

We had three horses on our farm. Frank and Charlie were Percherons, each weighing about two thousand pounds. Frank was named after our neighbor Frank Kolka, and Charlie was named after another neighbor, Charlie George. Frank and Charlie were calm and gentle and could be depended upon to do all the heavy work around the farm: pulling the sixteen-inch one-bottom plow, the disk, the smoothing drag, the corn planter and grain drill, the hay wagon, and the sulky cultivator used to cultivate the corn and potatoes to keep the weeds at bay. They were a matched pair, the same size and the same reddish brown color. And they got along well, not only when they were working but also when they were out on pasture or in the barnyard. If you saw one of them, you saw the other.

Then there was Dick, black as the night and just as mysterious. Dick was a mustang, meaning he had been born wild, corralled in the West, and shipped to the Midwest to be sold to an unsuspecting farmer who was accustomed to working with docile and much larger horses. Dick weighed about eight hundred pounds, less than half the weight of his stall mates. But he made up for his size with personality. He was filled with pride, always walking with his head high. And he was a loner. He wanted little if anything to do with Frank and Charlie, and Frank and Charlie ignored him.

While Frank and Charlie appeared to enjoy working, Dick seemed to remember his carefree days roaming the great Western plains with nary a concern in the world. While Frank and Charlie did the heavy pulling on the farm, Dick did the lighter work, such as pulling a one-row cultivator—a job he hated. And he let you know it, too. I often had the task of driving Dick on the one-row cultivator. To drive a horse on a one-row cultivator, you really needed four hands—two to guide the cultivator, and two to guide the horse. Since I had to grip the cultivator's two handles, I would tie the harness lines together and put them around my shoulders. Working this way, two hands ordinarily would be enough if you had a dependable horse, but Dick was far from dependable. No matter which field I happened to be working in, Dick always knew where the barn was—the place where he had water and hay and a chance to loaf. As he moved away from the barn, he plodded along, each step a bit slower than the previous one. When we got to the end of the row and made our turn, Dick could see the barn in the distance, and now suddenly he wanted to trot. I had all I could do to keep him in check before we once again got to the end of the row and turned around so Dick couldn't see the barn.

I both liked and disliked Dick's way of looking at the

world. I was never bored driving Dick; I paid attention, or I suffered the consequences. On the other hand, there often were days when I didn't want to pay attention. I had other things on my mind, maybe the neighbor girl or the upcoming threshing season with its good meals and great stories. There was no daydreaming when driving Dick—I had to stay on high alert at all times.

One time Dick's unpredictable nature caused a near catastrophe. It was a cool Saturday morning in November—butchering day. Bill Miller, our neighbor to the south, had come to help with the butchering, as he usually did. The killing was done in the hog yard, a few hundred yards from the shed where Pa had set up the barrel with boiling water used for scalding the carcass in order to loosen the hair so it could be removed. Once the killing was done, Pa's plan was to hitch Dick to the stone boat, roll the hog carcass onto the stone boat, and then drive to the shed, where the rest of the butchering would take place.

I noticed that Dick was doing a little high stepping and snorting as Pa pulled the stone boat up to the carcass. We rolled the carcass onto the stone boat, Pa said "gidup"—and at that moment Dick must have gotten a strong smell of blood. He reared up on his hind legs and took off across the barnyard, pulling the stone boat holding the dead pig and leaving Pa, Bill, and me behind to watch.

Pa had built a new barnyard gate the previous summer. He had painted it white, and it was beautiful, the best gate we'd ever had. Now Pa said, "There's no place for Dick to go—the barnyard gate is closed." What Pa had forgotten to factor in was that Dick was not a big, docile old draft horse but a nimble mustang longing for his days on the plains. As the horse reached the wooden gate, he slowed down not a whit but made a giant leap over it, topping the gate by at least a foot. Unfortunately, the stone boat carrying the pig struck the gate head on. With the crack of broken boards and wood flying in every direction, the dead pig rolled off the stone boat into the barnyard muck, and Dick continued on to the barn door. There he stopped, panting, not realizing—or caring about—the havoc he had just created.

I wanted to laugh; I had never seen a horse, any horse, jump over a barnyard fence. And watching that dead pig fly off the stone boat in midair—well, that had been something to see as well. But I knew better than to even smile as Pa ran to where the mustang now stood, its sides heaving. Pa yelled a few choice unprintable words at Dick before unhitching him from the stone boat and leading him into the barn.

Soon Pa reappeared, this time with Frank and Charlie. He hitched them to the mostly unharmed stone boat, and we rolled the dead pig back onto it. Butchering day continued. The story of the day that Dick jumped over the barnyard fence and spilled a dead pig would carry on down through the generations.

To Pa, Frank and Charlie were a part of our family, along with my mother and father, my brothers and me, and our farm dog, Fanny. Dick didn't quite make it into the family circle. But even when working with that ornery and unpredictable mustang, Pa's attitude was, "Respect the animals, and they'll respect you." When the team was doing heavy work, such as mowing hay or pulling the grain binder, at day's end he unharnessed the horses and watered and fed them before we went into the house for the evening meal. Caring for them always came first.

Many years later, when Pa bought a tractor, I asked him if he would be selling Frank and Charlie. "They'll never leave the farm," he said. When I asked why, he told me, "No matter how cold it is in winter, the horses will always start." But there was a deeper reason why Pa would never sell the horses. They were family.

I never came close to loving horses as much as Pa did. But I did learn from them. Each horse had its own personality, which I slowly learned and came to appreciate. Dick taught me that just because Frank and Charlie acted in a particular way did not mean all horses would act in the same way. Dick saw the world in his own way. Later, I would come to know dependable, hardworking people who were a joy to be around. But there was an outlier in almost every group, someone with his or her own way of doing things. Thanks to the lessons Dick taught me, I've enjoyed working with both kinds of people. I've often thought about the day Dick leaped over the barnyard fence when someone has "leaped over the barnyard fence" metaphorically, providing a break in an otherwise staid and predictable work setting.

Farm Dog

Fanny was a little ball of brown and white fur with a long, pointed nose. Pa had seen an ad in the *Wisconsin Agriculturist* and ordered the collie puppy from a kennel somewhere in southern Wisconsin. She arrived at the Wild Rose train depot one day in spring during the middle of the Great Depression, when I was too young to remember the details. But I do remember that Fanny grew rapidly into a full-size collie, standing about two feet tall at the shoulders and weighing fifty pounds or so.

From her first day on the farm, Fanny was Pa's dog. She wasn't a pet and was not allowed in the house except on winter days, when she curled up by the woodstove in the kitchen. She was never allowed in other rooms in the house. During most of the year, when she wasn't doing what was expected of farm dogs, she rested on a rug that Pa had provided for her on the kitchen porch. Her spot was out of the sun and on hot summer days was one of the cooler places on the farm.

Fanny was first and foremost a cow dog. That meant that one of her jobs was to fetch our small herd of cows from the pasture when it was time for the morning or evening milking. How Pa taught Fanny to do this will forever remain a mystery to me. I wish I had had enough sense to ask him about that, but I never did. Around five-thirty in the afternoon on a summer day, the pair would head toward the barn, Fanny walking beside Pa with her head held high and her big tail wagging. She had been waiting on the kitchen porch for the family to finish supper—she knew it was milking time without anyone having to tell her.

When they arrived at the barn, Pa would say, "Go fetch the cows, Fanny." That's all. One simple command. Fanny would trot off in the direction of the cow pasture, sometimes more than a half-mile from the farmstead. While she was gone, Pa and I would gather up the milking utensils from the combination pump house/milk house and wheel them into the barn on the wheelbarrow Pa had made just for that purpose.

By the time we had the milk cans and milk pails in place, in the distance we'd hear Fanny bark a couple of times. This told us that she was rounding up the cattle, urging those that were lying down to get up and get on their way to the barn, nipping at the heels of the occasional heifer that challenged her orders to leave the pasture, and urging the boss cow to start the group walking. The boss cow always led the way, with the rest of the cattle walking in single file behind her and Fanny in the rear, making sure there were no laggards.

I firmly believe that animal species communicate with one another. When the cows were in the barnyard, Fanny would often walk among them; they would put their noses down on her, and she would simply look at them in response. And I was sure Fanny and the boss cow had a special relationship. Without the boss cow leading the way, Fanny would have had a much more difficult time rounding up the cattle in the pasture.

Other than the twice-daily trip to the pasture at milking time, Fanny kept busy doing other jobs. For instance, Ma usually cared for one hundred or more laying hens that headquartered in the chicken house just west of the kitchen. A big old elm tree stood in front of the kitchen porch, a place where the family and visitors gathered on hot summer days. And when a stray chicken that had not yet been "trained" wandered under the shade tree and left an unwanted deposit, Fanny pounced on the unsuspecting bird and nailed her to the ground for a minute or two. Then she would let the hen up, and the offending bird would flap its way back to the chicken yard. The hen would lose a few feathers from the encounter, but otherwise Fanny didn't harm her. When the incident was over, Fanny would trot back to her resting place on the porch with what appeared to be a big smile on her face. That chicken would likely never again wander too close to the house. But another one would, and Fanny would have to once more teach a lesson.

Fanny never wore a collar, nor was she ever tied up. She was allowed to roam freely around the farm. We never called her a watchdog, but that was another of her roles. If a salesman of some stripe drove into the yard, Fanny would bark several times and trot out to the car to greet him. Salesmen who did not know about farm dogs might stay in the car, hoping that some human would appear and save them from the dog. Usually my mother watched all of this from the kitchen window, because Fanny's barking had alerted her to the visitor. If the salesman stayed in his car, Ma wasn't too sure she even wanted to talk with him, because he obviously had little knowledge of farmers and farm dogs. If he got out, said a few words to Fanny, and perhaps even patted the dog on the head, he at least got to talk with Ma. Fanny also was a watchdog for unwanted critters. If a fox had its eye on the laying hens and chose to make its move in the middle of a dark night, Fanny would raise such as ruckus that she would wake up Pa, who kept the double-barrel shotgun at the ready for such an occurrence.

Fanny was also a babysitter of the first order, watching over my brothers and me. Little traffic passed by our farm, but Fanny made sure that my twin brothers and I, when we were little guys, never got anywhere near the road simply by blocking our path.

When we kids were old enough to hunt squirrels, Fanny went with us. With twenty acres of oak woods just to the north of our farmhouse, we were but a few steps to good squirrel hunting. Oftentimes after I got home from school on a crisp fall afternoon, I'd grab my .22 rifle and head for the woods, Fanny alongside me. When I spotted a squirrel high up in an oak tree, the squirrel usually spotted me at the same time and quickly scurried around to the other side of the tree, so I could not get a shot. Fanny would trot around to the side of the tree where the squirrel was hiding and bark a few times, and the befuddled squirrel, now facing what appeared to be a dangerous barking dog, would move back around the tree, where I was poised to bag it. I have no idea how Fanny learned that skill.

In our human arrogance, we often believe that animals are here to learn from us. We fail to remember or refuse to accept that there is much we can learn from animals, especially from the smart ones. They also teach us in ways that are subtle, and silent: demonstrating respect for other animals, unconditional love for humans, trying their best to do what we want them to do, and often doing things for us that go far beyond our expectations.

Felix the Cat

Pa named the big tomcat Felix. Our cats, never allowed in the house, were of multiple colors and sizes. Little brown ones, midsize yellow ones, full-grown multicolored ones. A rainbow of cat colors added a splash of contrast to the dreary barn with its faded walls that needed whitewashing. Felix was completely black except for a pink nose and white-tipped tail. None of the other half-dozen or so barn cats had names, but this one did, and I assume my dad named him for the famous black and white cartoon cat.

Felix was friendly and mild-mannered. Unlike most of the other cats, he liked to have his back rubbed, and he seemed to enjoy people. He'd brush up against Pa's pant leg when Pa arrived in the barn and begin purring loudly as soon as Pa started doing chores. Another thing that set Felix apart from the other cats was his walk. No skulking around the corners and sneaking up to the milk dish that Pa provided for the cats; Felix walked proudly down the center of the aisle in back of the cows with his head up and his tail high. Maybe it was because of his size, or perhaps it was his demeanor, but the other cats stepped aside when Felix approached. No doubt about it, Felix was the boss cat in the barn.

When Pa bought a milking machine, the atmosphere in the barn changed. Before the machine, it had been quiet in the barn save for the sounds of cattle rustling their hay, horses munching grain, and calves jumping around in their pen. The new milking machine filled the barn with the *pop, pop* of the Briggs and Stratton engine running the vacuum pump and the wheezing of the milking machine units.

Felix was a curious cat. I doubt there was a corner of the barn—or the other farm buildings, for that matter—that he didn't know intimately. He took it upon himself to become acquainted with the noisy milking machine. The gasoline engine that ran the vacuum pump with a V-belt was located on a little platform just as you came in the barn door. The belt ran over two pulleys—a small one on the gasoline engine and a larger one on the vacuum pump.

I saw Felix standing beneath the engine and vacuum pump, looking up, his long black tail swinging back and forth. Not long after, I saw him on the platform, where there was just enough room for the big cat and the milking machine equipment. Soon this became his resting place while we milked. On cold winter days, the engine and the vacuum pump threw off enough heat to make it a cozy spot.

Pa anticipated what was going to happen. "That milking machine belt is gonna catch old Felix's tail one of these days," he would say. A couple of days later, I was working in the middle of the barn when I heard the most terrifying scream. I looked at the milking machine platform, and there was Felix, with all four legs extended straight out and his neck outstretched, sailing around and around as if something had him by the tail—which of course was the case. He had stuck his tail where no tail should go. By the time Pa got to the machine to shut it down, Felix had been flung against the wall. He stood up, dazed. He shook his head and then tore off at top speed under the cows, covering the entire length of the barn with a few mighty leaps. Upon reaching the end of the barn, he turned and headed down the aisle in back of the cows, yowling with each leap.

Pa yelled, "Open the door," which I did. Felix shot through the opening, bolted across the several hundred yards to the woods behind the house in seconds, and disappeared into the underbrush. We thought we would never see Felix again.

But we were wrong. A week later, Felix returned triumphantly. He paraded down the barn aisle with his head high and his tail raised. But now, rather than sticking out straight behind him, Felix's tail was bent in a right angle. As he walked south, his tail pointed west.

Animals, like people in their quest to be comfortable, can end up in trouble—getting their tail caught someplace where it shouldn't be. Luckily for Felix, his unfortunate accident didn't take anything away from his personality. He remained a proud cat, albeit one with a crooked tail.

Billy Goat Bob

Nobody seemed to know how Uncle Bud got himself a billy goat, but he did. Once he had it, he didn't know what to do with it. He called Pa.

"Was wondering if you have room for a billy goat on the farm," he asked. "Your boys would have fun with him. There's also a harness and a cart, the whole works."

Pa wasn't too sure he wanted another animal to add to the cows, pigs, chickens, and horses we already had. But he relented. "Bring him out to the farm," he finally said. The next day, Ross Caves, the local cattle trucker, drove into the yard. He climbed out of his truck with a big smile on his face.

"Got a billy goat for you, Herm," Caves said. "His name is Bob." The big white goat, sporting a white beard and two long curving horns, walked proudly down the truck ramp. When he reached the ground, he let out a big "Baaaaa," his way of saying hello, I supposed.

"Bud said to tell you that you can just let the goat loose—he won't run away, and then you don't have to worry about keeping him in a fence or finding a place for him in the barn," Caves said.

I led Bob to the house to show him to Ma. He stepped right up on the porch. Ma wasn't impressed. "Get that goat off the porch, or before you know it he'll be in the kitchen."

Bob and the goat cart did not get along. He either refused to pull it or he ran away with it. We quickly gave up on the cart.

We also discovered that Bob had some bad habits. Ma put a fence around her flowers, which kept Bob away. But then he turned to Ma's garden. Nobody messed with Ma's garden. One noon she told Pa that she was gonna shoot Bob if she ever caught him in her garden again. It was an idle threat, as Ma had never shot a gun in her life—but we all caught her message.

Pa was willing to put up with Bob's shenanigans when they involved Ma, but not long after the garden incident, Pa and Bob got personally involved. I was sitting on the porch, whittling on a stick and watching the goat out the corner of my eye. Pa had said I should keep an eye on the goat whenever I could so he didn't march back into Ma's garden. Pa was bending over, weeding the asparagus patch in front of the pump house. Bob was eating grass on the lawn, behaving himself as he had done all day. But what the goat saw was apparently too good to pass by. Noticing Pa bent over with his rump up in the air, Bob put his head down so his horns were like two car bumpers and he galloped toward Pa, who didn't hear him coming.

Whomp. I heard the sound clear as a bell. Pa went head over teakettle, dang near hitting the barnyard fence. It was quite the thing to see—and I couldn't help but burst out laughing. Pa got up, looked at Bob, and commenced to cuss. I couldn't recall when I'd heard a richer set of swear words coming out of Pa. He called the billy goat about every name I'd ever heard and lots I hadn't. The goat stood looking at Pa, shaking his head from time to time. I suspected Bob had been called names before. I knew that if Pa's shotgun had been handy, that goat would have been a goner.

Pa headed for the house. He walked right past me without saying a word. He went directly to the phone and rang up Uncle Bud.

"You can come and get your dang goat," Pa said. He was red in the face and breathing heavily.

The next day Ross Caves came for the goat and all of his equipment.

"Goat didn't work out?" Caves asked, grinning.

"Nope," Pa said. He wasn't grinning.

From billy goat Bob, I learned one important lesson. Never turn your back on a billy goat, especially one named Bob.

Peddling

I was always a shy little kid. Most of the time I wanted to be by myself rather than around other people, especially a lot of people. Both of my parents knew this. Pa had a tendency to like being alone, too, and farming provided lots of those opportunities, of course. But Pa also liked to be around others, especially small groups that included storytellers like himself.

Pa also liked talking to customers, as he did when he loaded up some of our home-grown fruits and vegetables and sold them house to house in the surrounding towns. My parents agreed that peddling, as Pa called this activity, might help me overcome my shyness. And so I began traveling with my dad when he peddled new potatoes (not difficult to sell, if they were large and free of blemishes) or fresh strawberries (also very popular).

We did so well, in fact, that Pa became confident that we could successfully peddle just about anything we grew on the farm. One year his confidence was severely challenged when we grew more than three hundred bushels of rutabagas hoping to sell most of them. We ate lots of rutabagas during our long winters, but two or three bushels covered our family's needs for a year. The remaining bushels were available for selling. Unfortunately, Pa had badly misjudged the rutabaga market. Where he thought his customers would quickly buy at least a bushel of rutabagas, we were lucky to sell someone one or two of the knobby tubers. Pa's theory that everybody liked rutabagas and that they were eager to buy home-grown ones was completely demolished.

But our peddling continued, year after year (though without a rutabaga offering after that first year), and I learned to overcome my shyness at least a little as I knocked on a town person's door and asked if they'd like to buy some fresh strawberries or potatoes.

By the time I was twelve or so, I had worked up enough courage to go out on my own as a salesperson. One of our farm magazines carried an ad that suggested kids could sell a special salve and earn credits toward a prize. "White Cloverine Brand Salve," the ad read. "Win a BB gun or a bicycle." With my hard-earned experience peddling farm produce, it would be easy to sell this special salve, I thought. All I had to do was sell a few tins of salve.

I tried to convince Ma that it was a good idea. I would sign up, I told her, and the company would mail me twelve tins of salve to be sold for twenty-five cents each. All I had to do was walk around the neighborhood and sell this outstanding product that soothed chapped hands, relieved minor burns, and helped heal cuts and bruises.

Ma was skeptical. She said that most people bought their

salve from the Watkins man, and they didn't need some fancy stuff that came in a little white tin with a picture of a clover on the lid. And besides, twenty-five cents was a lot of money for a small tin of the stuff, no matter how great it was.

I showed Ma pictures of the BB gun, jackknife, bike, and other impressive items available for prizes. "Look at this," I said. "All I gotta do is sell forty-eight tins, and a BB gun is mine."

"Don't you have to send in any money?" Ma inquired.

"Nope, you send in the money after you sell the salve. Says so right here." I tried to show her the ad while she was brushing butter on the tops of bread loaves she had just removed from the oven.

"I suppose it'll be alright," she finally said as she closed the oven door. "Wouldn't hurt to have some salve around here that didn't smell like disinfectant."

"Says Cloverine salve smells like clover," I said.

"We'll see."

A few days later, the rural mail carrier delivered a package to our mailbox. I ran up the driveway to the house and tore off the wrappings when I got into the kitchen. Here were the twelve tins of salve as promised. The cans seemed a lot smaller than those pictured in the ad, and I almost had to stick my nose in the salve to catch even a hint of clover smell. Ma took one sniff and said she couldn't smell any clover. I said she should take a bigger whiff, but she said she was too busy to waste her time smelling salve. She also noted, as I had, that the tins were a tad on the small side, especially when they were supposed to sell for a quarter each.

I developed my sales strategy. First I would walk over to the Alan Davis farm, only a half-mile away, then the Hudziak place, another half-mile, then three-quarters of a mile on to the Handrich farm, and a quarter-mile more to the Griff Davis place. My hope was that each would buy two or three tins, and soon I would be ordering more.

When I got home from my first selling trip, Ma asked how many tins I'd sold. I had to admit not one, but I said that I'd give it a try again the next day. Over the next several days, I managed to sell eight tins, including one to Ma and one to my Aunt Arvilla. But I had four more to go, and I was out of prospective customers. Now I was concerned about paying my bill to the Cloverine Company. Ma figured out that if I sent in the money I had taken in so far with the sale of eight cans, I would be free and clear. Thoughts of BB guns and bicycles disappeared from my mind. For a long time four tins of White Cloverine salve sat on the clock shelf in the dining room. I hoped that someone would stop by and ask what those four little tins with the clover design on the cover were. No one ever did.

Despite that disappointment, I continued helping Pa peddle farm produce. At least people didn't say disparaging things about our potatoes or strawberries, but of course I never forgot the rutabaga fiasco. I never knew (neither did Pa, apparently) that so many people disliked rutabagas, which we ate once or twice a week all winter long.

I discovered that selling is more complicated than merely showing people a product and hoping they will buy it. First I learned that the product must be something they wanted, or if they didn't, it was my job to convince them that they did. And the price had to be right. But no matter how good the price and how wonderful the product, some people will not buy. I learned to smile, say thank you, and move on to the next potential customer.

Finally, I learned that some people are just ornery. Perhaps they hated being bothered, or maybe their arthritis was kicking up the day I knocked on their door. "What do you want?" they would ask. I would explain what I was selling, using my best pitch. They slammed the door in my face. Another lesson learned.

Radio

Back in the days before TV, my family relied on our battery-powered radio for news, weather, and a large portion of our entertainment. Pa stretched an antenna (we called it an aerial) from the back of the radio through an upstairs window and on to the top of the windmill, and we could pick up Chicago and Milwaukee stations as clearly if they were just across the road. On cool, clear nights we picked up radio stations in St. Louis and Detroit and sometimes even Pittsburgh, which is where the first commercial radio station came on the air in 1920.

For my family, the radio was our main tie to the outside world. Much of early radio broadcasting was designed for farmers: early morning and noon market news, plus farming information from university researchers, and, of course, the weather. In addition, the University of Wisconsin's School of the Air made isolated country school kids part of a statewide group of students who tuned in together to learn more about nature, gain some practice singing, and learn about art, all by listening to the radio. The School of the Air was broadcast on WHA and WLBL, both operated by the University of Wisconsin in Madison. At my one-room country school, we tuned in our battery-operated radio and listened to the nature program *Afield with Ranger Mac*, the *Let's Sing* music program, and the *Let's Draw* art program.

At home in the evenings, my family enjoyed radio programs like *Amos and Andy, Fred Allen, Bob Hope, Lum 'n' Abner, The Jack Benny Program, Red Skelton, Milton Berle, Edgar Bergen and Charlie McCarthy, The Great Gildersleeve, The Life of Riley, The Aldrich Family*, and of course, *Fibber McGee and Molly*. No one wanted to miss Fibber McGee opening his overcrowded closet and having everything tumble out onto the floor (thanks to the wonders of sound effects) on nearly every episode.

We also liked *Gangbusters, The FBI in Peace and War, Death Valley Days*, and *The Shadow*, with Wisconsin boy Orson Wells playing the lead role of the Shadow. We enjoyed music programs like *The Guy Lombardo Show, Kraft Music Hall*, and *Your Hit Parade*, and variety shows including *Arthur Godfrey's Talent Scouts, The Ed Sullivan Show* (later on TV), and *Major Bowes' Original Amateur Hour*.

On Saturday nights, we listened to the *WLS Barn Dance* broadcast from the Eighth Street Theater in Chicago with Red Brand Fence (the Keystone Steel and Wire Company) as one of the major sponsors. It began broadcasting in 1924 and continued until 1960. Listening to the *Barn Dance* was the highlight of our week.

Soap operas were broadcast during daytime hours. My

mother sometimes listened to *The Romance of Helen Trent*, *Ma Perkins, Backstage Wife*, or *Our Gal Sunday*. But she was usually too busy with cooking, baking, mending, gardening, and taking care of the chickens to do much soap opera listening.

Every weekday afternoon, when my chores were done, I hurried into the house to listen to a program that came on the air about five. I had my choice of *Jack Armstrong, The Lone Ranger, Tom Mix, Terry and the Pirates, The Green Hornet, Sky King, Hopalong Cassidy, Tarzan, Sergeant Preston of the Yukon,* and *Captain Midnight.* They were fifteen-minute serials, which meant the story continued night after night. My brothers and I especially enjoyed *Tarzan,* and we altered his famous call "Tarzan of the Apes!" to "Tarzan of the Apps!" when we swung from ropes in the barn. But my favorite program of all was *Captain Midnight,* where the bad guys were captured, the good guys were saved, and everything turned out all right by the end of the segment.

These radio shows were a special treat after a long day at school followed by barn chores—especially on a cold winter afternoon. As I listened, I could picture the characters as if they were sitting there with me next to the radio. I lived their various exploits with them, worrying for them that they might fail or be hurt. Of course, they always came out on top. I wanted to be like that. I didn't tell anybody, but I longed to be like Jack Armstrong (the all-American boy) when I grew up. I wanted to be able to handle myself like

Captain Midnight did as he navigated the most calamitous situations with skill and clear thinking. Those radio characters were my heroes.

During those dark and sometimes dreary years before electricity and television came to the country, the radio played an enormously important role for me, for my family, and for our community. It connected us to the larger society, bringing us new ideas and new ways of understanding the world.

Guitar

Broadcast from Chicago every Saturday night, the *WLS Barn Dance* radio show featured an assortment of performers: Lulu Bell and Scotty, Red Blanchard, the Hoosier Hot Shots, and many more. The show was one of my family's favorites. The performers played beautiful music and sang songs in a way that set my standard for good singing. How I wished I could sing and play guitar like them!

Before my brothers and I were old enough to help with the heavy fieldwork, Pa employed a hired man each spring to work through the planting, growing, and harvesting season. The summer I was eleven, Pa hired Henry Lackelt. Henry, a tall, slim man in his early twenties, loved country music. When he arrived at our farm, he had a jacket, an old beat-up suitcase, and a guitar. This was the first time I'd seen a guitar up close. I was immediately reminded of the *WLS Barn Dance* and its guitar players, and I knew that I had to have a guitar of my own.

All summer long, in the evenings when the chores were done, we all gathered on the back porch and listened to

Henry strum on his guitar and sing. And what beautiful music it was: "That Silver-Haired Daddy of Mine," "Red River Valley," "Home on the Range," and many other songs. Sometimes we sang along with Henry, but mostly he sang by himself, while in the background we could hear the sounds of the early evening—crickets, an occasional owl hooting in the distance, and the sound of the neighbor's cowbell.

When fall rolled around and Henry prepared to leave, I dreaded his going. I wanted more than anything to have a guitar and be able to play like Henry. I'd been saving my money all summer, and I had accumulated something like three dollars. The day before he left, Henry took me aside and asked if I would like to buy his guitar.

"You bet I would," I said. "But all I've got is three dollars."

Henry rubbed his chin and thought for a minute. "How'd it be if I sold you this guitar for two dollars?"

"I'll take it," I said before even bothering to ask either Pa or Ma what they thought of the deal. With the dust not yet settled from the departure of Henry's old Model T Ford car, I began to strum on my wonderful instrument. But try as I might, the sounds that came from the guitar bore no resemblance to anything musical or anything like what Henry had produced when he played.

"Guess you're gonna have to take some music lessons," Ma said when she saw the disappointed look on my face. I hadn't thought about needing lessons to play the guitar. Henry had made it look easy.

Ma inquired around and learned that Mrs. Darling in Wild Rose gave piano and guitar lessons—fifty cents for an hour's instruction. The following week, on a Wednesday evening after the milking was done and I'd cleaned up a little, Pa drove me to Mrs. Darling's house.

I would like to report that taking music lessons with Mrs. Darling was a wonderful experience. It wasn't. She insisted that I learn how to read music. I tried to explain to her that I didn't care about reading music. I wanted to learn how to play my guitar. She said I had to do one before I could do the other. So I suffered along, complaining to Pa that all that I was learning was which letter stood for which note—stuff that had nothing to do with playing my guitar like the guitar strummers on the *WLS Barn Dance*. Pa pulled the plug on the whole deal after paying more for lessons than I had paid for my guitar.

I still have that guitar. And I still don't know how to play it—but one day I will, I hope. I didn't realize it at the time that some things require more than just the will to do them. Learning a new skill often requires instruction, plus hours of practice and the patience to keep trying. I never bothered to ask Henry Lackelt how he had learned to play. I should have.

Dancing

As a kid, I liked to listen to dance music, but I never knew the steps. I even read a book by Arthur Murray, the famous dance instructor, on how to dance. It was no help at all.

When I mentioned that I wanted to learn how to dance, one of my friends told me, "You're in trouble. You have to have a sister to show you how to dance." I had twin brothers. No sister. My brothers didn't know how to dance, either. I was stuck.

Another wise-guy friend told me that, to dance, you've got to feel the music. "Just gotta feel the beat," he said, "and then move your feet in time with it." That advice flew right over my head. I watched other people polka, do the old-time waltz, hop in time with the schottische, and then shuffle their feet around the dance floor when the music slowed. But I couldn't do any of it. I liked the music, but my feet didn't work.

I hate it when people offer a bunch of excuses as to why they can't or won't do something, so it is with considerable chagrin that I offer my best excuse for my dancing illiteracy. After having had polio at age twelve, I could hardly walk when I began high school at age thirteen in 1947. I never could run very well after that, and I walked with a slight limp. But that shouldn't have prevented me from learning to dance. I'd seen plenty of adults with limps dancing. Whatever the reason for their limp, they didn't use it as an excuse to stay off the dance floor.

By the time I was fourteen, I was becoming desperate. If you wanted to make an impression on a girl, you had to dance with her, at least the slow steps. I couldn't do the fast steps, the slow steps, any kind of steps. Pa told me, "Jerry, you seem to have two left feet," a comment that didn't help matters. But what did Pa know about dancing? Like me, he couldn't dance. Not a step. He never could, said he never would, and I believe he never did. He did offer me one piece of advice about dancing—not bad advice, either. "Girls don't like it when you step on their feet," he told me. I could understand that. I didn't like to have my feet stepped on either, though in my case it was usually a cow or a horse doing the stepping.

Now the junior prom was coming up. My junior class at Wild Rose High School had fifteen students, only four of them girls. The Grand March usually included four couples, which meant all four girls would participate. As a class officer (I was treasurer that year), I was expected to escort one of the girls to the prom and to be in the Grand March. No getting out of it.

I asked Joan Nordahl to be my date. A few days before the prom, I fessed up to Joan about my lack of dancing skills.

After she spent several noon hours teaching me basic dance steps, I was still having trouble meshing the beat of the music with the movement of my feet. Somewhere in that long string of connections between my brain and my feet, something had gone amuck. The music's beat either stayed in my brain or traveled to someplace in my skinny body where it got stuck. Yet somehow I made it through prom night without falling down or stepping too firmly on Joan's feet.

I kept practicing my dancing at school dances, and the connection from the beat of the music to my brain and my feet seemed to improve a little every time I did it. I moved on to more advanced dancing, including the polka and the old-time waltz and schottische. And somewhere along the way, I started to think that all of life is a kind of dance, where you hear the music and try to figure out the steps that allow you to dance to it.

Even farmwork was a kind of dance, I decided. I remember being small and trying to figure out just exactly what Pa meant when he gave me the briefest of demonstrations about hoeing potatoes. "This is what a little potato plant looks like," he said, pointing to one just emerging from the ground. "This is pig weed—see the difference?" I nodded my head, yes, but I wasn't sure I knew the difference. He went on pointing out weeds among the potatoes. "This is ragweed, this is purslane, this one's thistle—you see thistle only in the hollows—this is milkweed, and here is foxtail." This was the music, but what were the steps?

"Now here's how you get rid of these weeds." He used his trusty long-handled hoe to slice under the weed, avoiding the potato plant neatly, cutting the weed out of the ground. "If you just cover up the weed, it's gonna keep growing," he said. These were the dance steps that I must do, set to the music of what was a weed and what was a valuable plant.

I was maybe six or seven years old when I received the music of hoeing potatoes, with the appropriate dance steps properly demonstrated. But my young ears heard a mush of conflicting directions. *Hoe out the weeds. Don't touch the potato plants. Make sure you can tell a weed from a potato. Cut out the weeds, don't bury them.* The music was loud enough, but at first I couldn't catch the beat, couldn't figure out the dance steps. But slowly, with more "music" from Pa and with practice, practice, practice, I learned the steps. Eventually, hoeing became an easy dance—enjoyable, even (if hoeing can be said to be enjoyable)—as I found the rhythm.

As the years passed, there was more and different music to learn. When I was old enough to go out at night, neither Pa nor Ma said that I must be home at some specific time. Pa simply said, "I don't care how late you stay out, but you will be in the barn at five-thirty a.m. to help with the milking." I had to figure out my own steps to Pa's music. I quickly discovered that milking cows when you've had only a few hours' sleep is punishment of the highest order—without Pa ever saying that it was. Arriving home no later than eleven o'clock worked for me. I heard the music, got the beat, and figured out the steps.

As I've lived my life, that experience of learning to dance has proved invaluable. To this day, when I encounter something new, try a new skill, or attempt to wrap my mind around an idea that seems counter to my experience, I listen for the music, try to pick up the beat, and then learn the steps. It works for me, most of the time.

Stories

When I was growing up, storytelling was an integral part of life in our rural community. Whenever farmers got together, whether they were at the gristmill waiting for cow feed to be ground, around the table during threshing season, or over the back fence when they stopped their work for a chat, storytelling almost always resulted. Telling stories was a way for farmers to socialize, but more important, it was through stories that people shared their innermost thoughts, feelings, and emotions and found ways to relate to one another.

The most popular and effective stories had a humorous twist. Rural humor included practical jokes ranging from smearing Limburger cheese on the muffler of a newlywed couple's car to stuffing rocks in a grain sack so that the fellow carrying it from the threshing machine to the granary walked with a staggering gait and a look that said, "I've never carried such heavy grain." Or it might involve taking advantage of a city cousin who did not know the ways of the country, like when we told our four-year-old cousin that potato bugs were strawberries and that he should pick them and eat them. Or giving elaborate directions to a lost city soul when he only needed to travel a mile, turn right, and he would be back on the main highway. Or allowing a city-bred salesman to cower in his car while the farm dog stood barking at the car door—while the farmer knew that his dog was all bark and no bite.

Most rural storytellers stayed close to the facts, but they did embellish here and there, especially as time passed and the story was repeated. This was especially true of stories involving fishing and hunting. Other common stories I remember were about bad weather, ornery cows, runaway horses, and city farmers.

The vast majority of the stories were humorous, although the subjects and the situations were generally far from funny. Humor was a way of making a bad situation better, of finding something good in something that was awful, of evoking laughter in a time filled with tears—stories about a farmstead fire, a charging mad bull, or a tipped-over pickup truck; stories about minor (or not so minor) injuries caused by poor judgment or lack of knowledge.

Most communities, including mine, had at least one storyteller who was especially adept at inventing facts and situations and weaving them into the most outrageous stories. We enjoyed these yarns even though we all knew they held not a smidgeon of truth. Of course these "truth inventors" also became the subject of stories. "Did you hear the story that Bill told last week about the mountain lion he saw in his backyard?" Other people merely dismissed Bill's stories:

"You just can't believe a word that old Bill says. He's an out-and-out liar."

Several people in our community were good with one-liners. For example, "Never buy a horse that is blind in one eye and can't see out of the other." If I asked a neighbor, "How you doing today?," I might get a one-line response: "I was born with nothing and I have most of it left." Or, "I'm feeling a lot better than I ought to for a person of my age."

Here are some other one-liners, many spoken by my father at one time or another:

- When you are doing nothing, how do you know when you are finished?
- Just because you've got a lot of education doesn't mean you know anything.
- No matter what direction a north wind comes from, it always blows cold.
- If bigger is better, why is a dime worth more than a nickel?
- It's all right to not have anything to say as long as you don't say it.

Humor helped country people through the tough times, when the rains didn't come and the crops dried up, when a friend or relative died, when milk prices fell, or when someone in the family was injured. Country humor was home-made; it was of the people. It was humor that came from the land. And whether it evoked a belly laugh or only a chuckle, it cheered people up—and often had a deeper message or meaning that transcended the story. For country people, good weather nourished their crops; humor nourished their souls.

The following story was long retold in our community. Griff Davis, our neighbor to the east, decided it was time to paint his barn. He and his hired man, John, were making good progress with the painting when they came upon a huge hornets' nest high up in the barn's peak. The hornets had to be removed before the men could continue painting. But how would they remove them without getting stung? Griff had a plan.

"John, go to the house and fetch me some old rags," he instructed. While John was off fetching the rags, Griff located an old broomstick and a jug of kerosene. When John returned with the rags, Griff wrapped them around the broomstick, soaked the rags with kerosene, and touched a match to them. Immediately flames shot out from the burning rags. The plan was a good one. Hornets would disperse when confronted with a smoky, flaming torch.

"Here," Griff said, quickly handing the blazing torch to John. "Skin up that ladder and touch the flames to the nest. That'll scare off them stingin' buggers."

John did as he was instructed, holding the flaming torch well away from the ladder as he quickly climbed to where he could reach the hornets' nest. John was not prepared to deal with what happened next.

As he leaned out from the ladder, trying to position the flaming torch of loosely wrapped rags under the hornets' nest, Griff's sow pig walked under the ladder, unaware of what was taking place thirty feet above her. A gust of ill-timed wind caught the end of the torch, and a hunk of burning cloth about the size of a bandana landed squarely on the back of the big white sow. At that moment, the well-crafted plan for removing hornets went completely awry.

The surprised pig let out a loud *Umph* and ran toward the straw stack, likely believing she needed to protect her litter of little pigs that were housed in a shelter Griff had built under the stack. Griff saw what was happening, and quickly he crawled under the straw stack after the enraged pig. John, who had nearly fallen as he scrambled down the ladder, was soon crawling after Griff. Griff had visions of the straw stack going up in flames and with it the barn, which was just a few feet away. John was concerned that he would be blamed for allowing the flaming cloth to fall from the torch on the big white sow.

Halfway in to where the little pigs were located, the now only smoldering piece of cloth fell off the sow in front of Griff, who quickly snuffed out the remaining embers. Now the danger shifted.

When the sow determined that she was being followed, she declared the followers her new enemy. She turned, let out a big grunt, and charged Griff, who now lay flat, covering his head with his arms as the sow ran over him on her way toward John. John did the same thing. There was little damage to either of the men, except for some hog tracks on their backs. Griff noted the burn damage to the old sow was minimal, as she began rooting once more in the barnyard.

John and Griff sat by the barn and discussed a new, less dangerous strategy for removing the hornets, which were now thoroughly agitated and flying all about. They wouldn't laugh about what had happened under the straw stack until much later.

Life on the farm could be dangerous, even devastating. But when things turned out as they did in this story, the tale became one that was told again and again as farmers gathered at the feed mill, the cheese factory, or the local tavern. If you listened carefully, almost every story, even the funniest or most outrageous, had something important to say. Stories are like that.

Farmer Talk

Those of us who grew up on farms during the years I did learned a special language. I call it "farmer talk." For instance, when I hear a reference to cows being fed *food*, I cringe. We did not feed cows *food*; we fed them *feed*. We feed people food. *Feed* is an example of the many words that we used that were both nouns as well as verbs. Another is *mow*. When pronounced rhyming with "how," it refers to the place where hay is stored in a barn: the haymow. When the word is pronounced to rhyme with "flow," it means the process of cutting hay or grass.

Planting crops has a special language as well. Farmers plant corn. But when we put oats in the ground, we call it seeding. And we plant potatoes, but what we plant is a potato seed.

The word *make* is used in multiple ways on the farm. When we went to the woodlot in back of the farmhouse to cut down trees for firewood, we called the activity "making wood." When we harvested hay, we called it "making hay."

And when times were tough and our opportunities were limited, we called it "making do."

Most folks in our farming community also used unique phrases, many of them with farm flavor, that had particular meanings:

"At the end of your rope": You are out of options.

"Barking up the wrong tree": Looking in the wrong place for a solution.

"Can't cut the mustard": Not up to the job at hand.

"The cat's meow": Said about something great—or, sarcastically, about someone who thinks highly of himself or herself.

"Clean as a whistle": Absolutely clean.

"Dead as a doornail": Absolutely dead.

"Face that would stop a clock": A homely person.

"Full of wind": Someone who talked a lot but didn't say anything.

"Windbag": See *Full of wind.*

"Hold your horses": Wait a minute.

"Keep your shirt on": Be patient.

"Lickety-split": Very quickly.

"Bat out of hell": Even faster than lickety-split.

"Nailed down": Something difficult is figured out.

"Neck of the woods": Specific geographic area.

"One-horse town": A place with limited resources.

"Pickled": Someone who has spent too much time at the village tavern.

"Put one over": To get the upper hand, to best someone.

"Putting on the dog": Showing off, often with the kind of clothing worn.

"Rule the roost": To be in charge.

"Scarcer than hen's teeth": Something that can't be found.

"Snookered": Cheated out of something.

"So skinny she doesn't cast a shadow": Thin.

"So tight he squeaks": Overly frugal.

"Strange duck": An unusual person.

"Take a hike": Time for you to leave.

"Take the bull by the horns": Take charge of a situation.

"Tall drink of water": A tall person.

"Too big for his britches": Someone filled with self-importance.

"Tough as nails": Someone able to continue with a difficult job.

"Two shakes of a lamb's tail": Soon.

"Under the weather": Not feeling well.

"Until the cows come home": Waiting a long time for something to happen.

"Up a tree": Not knowing which way to turn.

"Were you born in a barn?": Asked when someone entered a house and didn't close the door.

"Whistle another tune": Changing one's mind.

"Works like a horse": A hard worker.

"You can just come to hell": Spoken in a fit of anger by someone who has difficulty keeping his verbs straight or who is looking for a companion to join him where he believes he already is.

As a farm kid, I learned the names for the various ages and sexes of animals, which often confuse many urbanites. For instance, a pig is not just a pig, although a pig can be called a hog when it is mature (and not because it eats a lot). A mature female pig that has given birth to a litter of pigs is called a sow. A mature male pig is a boar (not because he is boring). A gilt is a female pig who hasn't given birth. A barrow is a castrated male pig that is raised solely for meat production. Little pigs can be called piglets or merely little pigs. Feeder pigs are of either sex, weigh about 40 pounds, and are sold to farmers who feed them until they reach market weight, which is about 250 pounds. And when you buy lard in the store, it comes from pigs, as do hams, pork loins, and pork chops.

Driving in the countryside, we often see "cattle" grazing in the field. There is a fundamental difference between beef cattle (raised for meat) and dairy cattle (raised for milk). These days, one is more apt to see beef cattle than dairy cattle on pasture, as the larger dairy farms keep their dairy cows inside throughout the year.

Not every dairy animal is a cow. Cows are female, they give milk, and they have given birth to one or more calves. Female calves are called heifers and remain heifers until they give birth. Male calves and mature males are bulls. A steer is a castrated male. The term *dairy cattle* refers to all categories: cows, bulls, heifers, calves, and steers. Beef cattle have the same categories as dairy cattle. The word *herd* refers to a collection of dairy or beef animals.

A female sheep that has given birth is a ewe, pronounced "you." A baby sheep is a lamb. A mature male sheep is called a ram or a buck, and a castrated ram is a wether, pronounced "weather."

Female goats that have given birth are called does. A male goat is a buck, and the babies are called kids. A female horse that has given birth is a mare, the offspring is a foal (either male or female), and a mature male is a stallion or a stud. A filly is a young female horse; a gelding is a castrated male horse.

To be accepted by any community and to truly understand that community, one needs to speak its language. For those of us with rural roots, remembering the language allows us to remain connected to rural communities and rural people, something that I prize today as I work with people from both rural and urban places.

Winter Fun

We had a lot of winter in our part of Wisconsin, usually settling in around the middle of November and often staying with us into early April. Winter sports were important to me and my brothers. We skated, built snow forts and snow caves, organized snowball fights, and made snowmen. At recess we played fox and geese, a game of tag with paths made in the snow. I tended to my trap line each morning on skis, and of course we downhill skied for the sheer fun of it.

When I was four or five, Pa made my first pair of skis out of barrel staves, the curved slats from wooden barrels that were about three feet long. He nailed a thin strip of leather onto each stave for my rubber boots to fit into. I didn't mind much that my barrel-stave skis were clumsy and performed poorly on hills. They served just fine on level ground, sort of like snowshoes.

A couple of years later, my grandfather Witt made me a pair of skis from two five-foot strips of birch wood that he steamed over a teakettle until he could bend up the front ends. He also nailed a strip of leather across the middle of each of them to accommodate my four-buckle rubber boots. They were wider than barrel staves, and with the turned-up ends I could sail down the hills as well as any kid with store-bought skis. Unfortunately, the skis Grandpa made did not have grooves cut in the bottom to keep them going straight. If the snow was packed, I would as likely go sideways as straight ahead—an added benefit that I pointed out to my friends who had "better" skis.

When I was ten, I received a pair of factory-made skis for Christmas. Pa bought them at Hotz's Hardware in Wild Rose. They were seven feet long, with a strip of leather to hold my now six-buckle rubber boots. These skis had two grooves on the bottom of each for superior control and steering. Each ski, somewhere along the way, had lost its mate. One ski was black, the other brown. Dad painted the brown one black to make the two discarded skis into a pair. With my new skis I skied to school, skied my trap line each morning, skied to neighbors, and skied at skiing parties the neighborhood kids organized. Somewhere in the shed at my farm I still have one of these old skis. Its mate broke years ago when I hit a stone, or maybe it broke when I got tangled up in a wire fence I tried to cross. The remaining ski, alone again, has many stories to tell.

With winter dragging on and often intensifying in January, how my brothers and I enjoyed the brief respite that Pa called a woodpecker thaw. It usually came in mid-January after days of bitter cold and deep and drifted snow. It often arrived overnight, while my brothers and I slept in the cold upstairs bedroom in our drafty farmhouse.

We knew the winter thaw had arrived when the eaves on the house started dripping, which I noticed when I hurried to the barn for the early morning milking. By midmorning it began to rain—a slow, steady, snow-melting rain. Throughout the day, my brothers and I kept watch on the big hollow in front of the house, where the snow turned from white to gray and then to meltwater as the hollow became a pond.

With the pond slowly becoming larger, I looked for my ice skates, the clamp-on-your-shoes type that I tightened with a little key that I carried in my pocket. I had hung the skates in the woodshed the previous spring and forgotten about them until the thaw arrived.

The thaw disappeared quicker than you could say, "Isn't that a north wind blowing this evening?" Freezing weather returned, but the pond remained. A beautiful, flat slippery surface made for three boys and their clamp-on skates their pa had bought at Hotz's Hardware for fifty cents a pair.

The pond would remain perfect for ice-skating, sometimes for several weeks. Then a major snowstorm would bury it, and unless we wanted to do a lot of shoveling, our skating season was over. Our skating pond was another gift of winter for boys who'd tired of shoveling snow, carrying wood, and doing all the other winter-required jobs. Being able to ice skate just a hop and a skip from our farmhouse is one of those small pleasures that I've never forgotten.

The Mercantile

Every Saturday, our family traveled to Wild Rose in our 1936 Plymouth so Ma could shop at the Mercantile. We went in the evening during the warmer months, in the afternoons in winter. We missed the trip only if it was storming or if the roads were blocked with snow.

Wild Rose, population around 550, was four and half miles east of our farm. The Plymouth's heater, never adequate even on moderate days, failed miserably if the temperature slid below zero. My brothers and I snuggled under thick car blankets to keep warm as we motored along, usually at not more than twenty-five miles an hour. When we reached County Highway A, about a mile south of our farm, Pa turned east and we picked up a little speed, as the county road was plowed wider. The Plymouth struggled up to thirty miles an hour (in summer its top speed was fifty); any faster than that and it shook and shimmied like it might fly into pieces.

At the Wild Rose Mercantile, Ma traded her eggs for groceries; sometimes she got some money back, and occasionally she had to pay a little more in cash. The Mercantile was a two-story brick building owned and operated by Arnol Roberts, a slightly built man, and his equally slightly built wife, Dorothy. The building had multiple purposes. Upstairs was the dance hall, where people danced the polka at wedding receptions, birthday parties, or anniversaries. That is, until one Saturday night when customers on the first floor noticed that the ceiling light fixtures were swaying to the music. A state inspector came by, and there were no more polka dances upstairs.

Next to the dance floor was a dentist's office, reached by climbing an outside iron fire escape. Everything was painful about a visit to the dentist, including the long, scary climb to his office.

In the basement were two bowling lanes, left unused since a bowling alley had been built next door. But for me, the most important feature of the basement was the collection of books found there—all hardcovers, selling for forty-nine cents apiece. Mr. Roberts often led me down to look at them. He knew I was interested in reading and that I had few books at home. I saved my money, and every month or so I paged through his wonderful collection—*Treasure Island, Swiss Family Robinson, Little Men, Little Women, The Black Arrow, Alice's Adventures in Wonderland*—and listened to Mr. Roberts's recommendations about which one I should buy. I still have those books on my bookshelf.

The first floor of the Mercantile was essentially a large department store. There was a clothing department, with racks of barn coats, OshKosh B'gosh bib overalls, flannel shirts for winter, thin cotton shirts for summer, straw hats, and winter caps, the best ones with cat-fur earlaps. On a wall to the left of the clothing, boxes of shoes were stacked higher than even Mr. Roberts could reach. They were mostly work shoes, Wolverine brand, with tops that reached above the ankle. Scattered among the rows of work shoes were a few low-top shoes, the kind people wore to church, to weddings and funerals, and to polka dances. Rubber boots were stacked next to the shoes, the smell of new rubber almost overpowering the smell of new leather. Customers could buy two-buckle boots, four-buckle boots, and best of all, six-buckle boots. The more buckles, the higher the boots and the deeper the barnyard muck that could be waded through without getting wet feet. Next to the rubber boots were the barn rubbers, the kind I pulled over my shoes when I went for the cows on a dewy morning.

Here and there stacked on shelves and piled on top of everything else were toys: dolls, teddy bears, wagons, sleds, card games, and checkerboards. Around Christmastime, Mr. Roberts brought the toys together in one spot so that shoppers didn't have to look all around the store for the one they wanted.

The dry goods department was found on the wall opposite the shoes. Piled on shelves were bolts of cloth that Mrs. Roberts unrolled for Ma so she could choose material for a dress, for shirts for my brothers, or for an apron for Aunt Minnie, whose birthday was coming up. With the selection made, Mrs. Roberts tore off the proper length of cloth, neatly folded it, wrapped it in brown paper, and strung a length of white string around it in both directions.

The grocery department was on the far end of the store. Behind the grocery counter were stacks of cornflake and oatmeal boxes, cans of pork and beans and tomato soup, tins of sardines, canned red salmon from some far-off place I had never heard of, and more. Ma handed her grocery list to Mr. or Mrs. Roberts, who went looking for what Ma wanted and brought it back to the counter. The groceries were stacked in Ma's egg crate. Then, with the grocery shopping completed, we drove back home, already looking forward to repeating the event the next Saturday.

Going to town for a couple of hours a week was one of the simple things that I so much enjoyed doing. By watching my mother trade for groceries and other items, I learned about money—how little of it we had, and how important it was to save some of what little I did have.

Catalog

Twice a year, in spring and fall, the Sears, Roebuck catalog arrived in our mailbox. We all watched for its arrival. On the catalog's pages was everything our farm family could possibly want or need, and we could obtain these items simply by filling out an order form, writing a check, and mailing it in. In a few days, we could expect the product to arrive in our rural mailbox—unless it was a larger item such as a wagon, a bedroom dresser, or even a barn or a house, which would be shipped to the closest railroad depot.

Sears, Roebuck and Company produced its first catalog, offering watches and jewelry, in 1893. By 1896, the catalog was mailed twice a year to nearly every rural household throughout the country and included not only watches and jewelry but sewing machines, sporting goods, musical instruments, firearms, buggies, bicycles, baby carriages, and clothing.

Small-town storekeepers, especially those who carried similar items, were furious. It's easy to see why. Rural people quickly came to enjoy the wide variety Sears offered—with many more choices than found in their local stores—and the convenience of delivery straight to their mailboxes. The catalogs had a second use; during the years before farmers had indoor plumbing, many of them were recycled to the outhouses, serving as free toilet paper.

In 1908, Sears began offering house plans in its catalog. Starting in 1915, one could order an entire precut house. By 1911, Sears offered barn plans, and a few years later, the catalog included plans for hog houses, corncribs, and chicken coops. From 1918 to 1930, Sears offered an all-barn catalog called *The Book of Barns*. From this catalog, a farmer could order an entire precut barn in one of seven styles. Prices ranged from $1,316 for a smaller barn to $3,807 for a larger one. After ordering, the farmer waited for the local depot agent to call and inform him that his barn had arrived.

My copy of the spring and summer 1940 Sears, Roebuck catalog includes 1,042 pages of items, each one enticingly described, with the price and shipping weight noted. The first pages of the catalog feature women's dresses, describing the newest ones as "Young and Carefree Fashions ... the Story of 1940. A black dress, elegance personified in this dramatic princess dress, new as this minute." That dress cost $5.98. The newest offerings are followed by 191 pages of women's clothing, including hats and accessories, plus two pages of umbrellas priced from $1.00 to $2.89. (We never owned an umbrella; Pa said they were for city people. When it rained, we mostly got wet.)

Other items in the 1940 catalog include books (from Steinbeck's *Grapes of Wrath* for $2.75 to Hitler's *Mein*

Kampf for $3.00); six pages of cameras, ranging from $1.79 for a box camera to $29.70 for an Argus 33-mm slide camera; sixty-six pages of farm equipment, including a crosscut saw ($4.45), kerosene barn lantern ($1.39), steel-wheeled hay wagon ($41), windmill ($29.90), two-row horse-drawn corn planter ($52.50), leather horse harnesses ($41.90), and much more.

Shortly after Thanksgiving each year, my brothers and I began watching for the mailman to arrive at our farm mailbox in his blue car. Clarence Corning was his name, and you could set your watch by his arrival at eleven o'clock each morning.

We were patiently waiting for the arrival of the Sears, Roebuck Christmas catalog, the "wish book," as everyone called it. When it came, we spent most of the time when our chores were done and our homework finished poring over its pages. Page after page of toys—Tinker Toys, Lincoln Logs, board games, dolls, BB guns, yo-yos, windup trains, teddy bears, and books. The wish book featured clothing, too, but we were more interested in the toys than the clothing. For Christmas each year we were allowed to pick one toy and one piece of clothing. I usually selected a book and a sweater or a plaid flannel shirt.

I especially remember 1946, for that fall we had been wired for electricity. For our 1946 Christmas present, my mother ordered a metal erector set for the three of us boys to share. With the erector set we could build windmills, steam shovels, and cranes. The set included a little electric motor. But we had to wait until the following April, when our electricity was finally switched on, to plug in the motor and power the wonderful machines we had created.

Sears produced its first Christmas catalog in 1933; the company continued to publish a print version until 1998. For us old-timers, a little bit of Christmas disappeared when we no longer found the Sears wish book in our mailboxes a few days after Thanksgiving.

For me, those Sears, Roebuck catalogs provided an education about the material culture of the United States (although I surely wouldn't have used those words at the time). I could see what other people were wearing, what new books were available, and what conveniences people had in their homes, especially those who had electricity. I learned what was new in farm equipment and the cost of a new ax. Most special of all, for a farm kid, was the annual Christmas catalog. Even though for us most of the items were there only to be looked at, they offered an opportunity to wish, to dream, and to imagine.

Mischief

McKinley Jenks, whose farm was the closest one to our Chain O' Lake country school, had a contract with the town of Rose to grade the gravel roads in the township using his team of horses and the township's rusty old road grader. He began grading roads after the spring thaw.

All the recess games in the schoolyard stopped as Jenks, his team, and the grader began climbing the little knoll in front of the school. The small gray horses strained in their harnesses as the grader rolled up a heavy thread of gravel in front of the shiny blade. Mac, as everyone knew him, took his hands off the controls of the machine to wave at us as we lined up along the fence to watch the team and the grader move by.

We could smell the sweaty horses and the freshly turned gravel, not unpleasant aromas to farm kids accustomed to smells of the land. When the horses and grader were close to the schoolhouse gate, one of the older boys began jumping up and down and waving his handkerchief. The rest of us soon joined in this mischief, having no idea of the likely consequences.

Mac Jenks's horses were good workers but a bit skittish. When they saw our animated group with handkerchiefs waving, they reared on their hind legs, their front legs pawing the air. Mac struggled to control the team, alternatively yelling "whoa" to the horses and "stop it, you kids" to us.

Mac was never known for polite language, even when women and children were around. Next, a stream of invectives gushed out of his mouth, words that many of us had never heard before, even those of us who prided ourselves on knowing the popular cuss words of the day.

We stood wide-eyed as the horses continued to rear and their driver tried to control them, now alternately cussing us and the out-of-control team. One of the horses slipped and fell on the road grader's tongue, the wooden pole that separated the team while they were hitched to the grader. The tongue snapped with a sound like a rifle shot, and the team stopped thrashing. For a moment there was silence. My classmates and I stood with our mouths open. Not one of us could have imagined that our little fun would have such devastating results.

When Mac discovered the damage that had been done and realized that this was the end of road grading for the day, the stream of cuss words increased in intensity. Many of the younger children had already run into the schoolhouse, hoping that the building would shield them from this man who seemed to have lost control. We older students knew that

Mac couldn't physically harm us because he could not leave his team of frightened horses and the broken road grader.

The bell rang twice, and we all hustled into the schoolhouse, leaving Mac to contend with the problem that we had created. On the way into the school building, I heard Jim Steinke say, "Geez, that Mac Jenks sure can swear, can't he?" I agreed.

We had no more than gotten into our seats when our teacher said she wanted to talk about what had happened outside. She said one of the second-graders had come to her and said, "A man with wild horses is outside, and he is swearing loudly."

She managed to extract from us exactly what happened and said that we had to stay inside during the noon hour and there would be no recess for any of us that afternoon. But that wasn't the end of it.

That evening, when I had finished the barn chores and was doing my homework, Mac Jenks drove into our yard. He had calmed down some but was still clearly angry. He told Pa what had happened and that I had been a part of the mischief. Pa offered to make a new tongue for the road grader—and guess who did most of the work making that tongue?

My brother Darrel had been watching a pair of red-headed woodpeckers build a nest in an old, hollow apple tree not far from the pump house. After a few days, he figured the nest must be built and the eggs laid. He wondered what a red-headed woodpecker's eggs were like. How big were they? What color? His ten-year-old brain came up with a plan. When he saw the woodpecker leave the hole in the old apple tree, he would reach in and pick up one of the eggs he assumed was there and examine it. He already knew about the eggs of robins and several other birds, but he wanted to add the red-headed woodpecker egg description to his knowledge. Then he could really impress his friends at the country school with something that he bet they didn't know.

So he stood back watching and waiting for the woodpecker to leave the nest. His twin brother, Donald, stood nearby, also interested in what the nest would reveal.

Finally the woodpecker left the nest and flew off. Confidently, Darrel walked to the old apple tree with a hole in its side and thrust in his arm, farther and farther, hoping to reach the nest and the eggs that he knew must be there. Donald watched from a safe distance away.

Then Darrel felt the most excruciating pain. Something bit into his hand. He quickly removed his arm from the hole; blood trickled down his hand. He had forgotten that woodpeckers take turns sitting on the nest. One of the pair was at home, and she wasn't about to let any foreign enemy get close to her eggs.

Donald stood to the side laughing. "Bet you won't do that again," Donald said.

Junior Osinski, another farmer in our neighborhood, had a green Oliver tractor that he bought brand new. There was nothing he thought more of. He kept his tractor so well shined that you could see your face reflected off the hood. At the end of a day plowing, disking, or cultivating, Junior always took time to wipe off the dust and grime that had accumulated on the machine. Junior and the tractor he kept looking as shiny and new as the day he bought it were the talk of the neighborhood.

During threshing time the summer when I was seventeen, my brother Don and his friend Marvin Miller decided they would pull a trick on Junior and his shiny tractor. He's asking for it, the boys reasoned. We were threshing at the Osinskis' farm, and we'd all filed into the house for the noon meal. I noticed that Don and Marvin left the table a little early, but that wasn't unusual. Some of the guys often got up and left before the rest finished their pie and coffee.

It was a warm day in August, sunny with no hint of a breeze. A good day for threshing because the dust didn't fly around and the straw stayed put when it was blown on the straw stack. After a big dinner, we all gathered under a maple tree, resting in the shade and spinning stories of other threshing days. Junior's shiny green Oliver stood off to the side, near one of the bundle wagons. He'd unhitched it from the wagon before dinner for some reason and now needed help to re-hitch.

Junior climbed onto the seat of his shiny tractor while Pa held the tongue on the bundle wagon. Junior had no sooner pushed the starter button when a high-pitched whistle came from under the tractor's hood, followed by a huge cloud of black smoke that hung over the machine like a thunder cloud.

Pa yelled, "It's gonna blow up!" He took a step backward and fell over the wagon tongue. He crawled on his hands and knees away from the doomed machine. Meanwhile, Junior leaped off the tractor seat and ran for maple tree where everyone was now standing watching the whistling, smoking tractor.

Junior had just made it under the tree when there was a loud *ka-boom* and more black smoke.

"I think your tractor's a goner," Bill Miller said.

"We'd better find some water and put out the fire before it causes more damage," somebody else offered.

But there was no fire. And soon there was no more smoke. Don and Marvin stood with the rest of the onlookers, keeping serious, concerned looks on their faces. Slowly Junior walked toward his tractor.

"Be careful, Junior," Don yelled, keeping a straight face. "Might blow up again."

Junior eased forward a step at a time. I could see that he was ready to sprint away if he heard or saw the first inkling of another blast. Pa stood off to the side, brushing straw and dirt from his overalls. He'd lost his straw hat when he fell over the tongue and was waiting to find out if it was safe to retrieve it.

Slowly, Junior walked around his shiny tractor, which was a little smudged here and there from the black smoke. Then he snapped open the hood and found the remnants of a prank smoke bomb, the kind that could be ordered from a catalog and that newly married couples often found in their autos. The device did no damage other than making a lot of noise and creating a huge cloud of black smoke.

"Damn smoke bomb," Junior said, pulling off the wires and throwing them on the ground in disgust.

Everybody under the maple tree began laughing, all except Junior, who was mad, and Pa, who was even madder.

"When we find out who did this, there's gonna be hell to pay," Pa said. He was red in the face and trying to keep his false teeth in place. (Whenever he got excited, his false teeth came loose.)

But Pa didn't find out then. Neither did Junior, until years later when Don and Marvin confessed their deed. Junior laughed when he heard. Pa didn't.

Lessons learned. What might appear to be a simple prank—waving a handkerchief at a team of horses or attaching a smoke bomb to a neighbor's tractor—can have unintended consequences. Also, don't poke your hand in a dark hole, no matter how curious you might be. Mischief can be a great teacher—of what *not* to do.

Peas

When I was growing up, when we did farmwork away from the farm we called it "working out." When I was old enough, I worked out at the cranberry bog and the pea cannery. I learned valuable lessons at both.

In several areas in southern and eastern Wisconsin, farmers grew peas as a cash crop, selling their harvest to nearby commercial canneries. For two summers in the early 1950s, I worked for the California Packing Company in Markesan. The first year, I stacked box after box of canned peas in the warehouse, starting at seven in the morning and working until past midnight before falling onto my cot in the bunkhouse to catch a few hours' sleep and then doing it all again the next day. We worked seven days a week during the canning season, which ran from mid-June until late July, depending on the weather and the quality of pea crop that season.

The next summer I was promoted to viner boss. The California Packing Company stationed several pea viners near where the peas were grown, including one about four miles north of Markesan. The viner was a large wooden machine, ten feet or so tall, with a rotating drum that separated the peas from the vines and shucked them. The viner was covered with a roof, but the ends and sides were open. A Farmall M tractor engine in a nearby lean-to powered the viner. My job was to supervise the crew and keep the engine and the viner running—no small task, as the viner was old, and nearly every day something either fell apart or broke.

The crew consisted of a man from Jamaica, a hardworking, easy-to-get-along-with fellow; a high school teacher from Markesan who needed a summer job; and a third fellow, the oldest of the group, maybe in his fifties, and, I soon found out, an alcoholic. When he was sober he worked hard, but when he was drunk he was a menace to himself and everyone else.

Our tasks were as follows: pitching a tangle of pea vines into the front of the machine, boxing the shucked peas that came out the back end of the machine, moving the spent pea vines around to create a stack, and weighing and recording the number of pounds of peas each farmer delivered. The latter was my job; the other jobs rotated among the workers. Pitching the peas into the machine was the most difficult, and I tried to rotate the men so no one had to pitch for more than an hour at a time.

After only a few days of operation, I noticed that the older man was consistently drunk by noon, and I feared having him work around the viner machine. I assigned him to working on the pea stack. But I continued to wrestle with what to do about him. In the morning, when he was sober, he was a good worker. By afternoon I wanted to fire him, but I really couldn't because we needed a full crew now, and all the hiring was done at the main office in Markesan. So one early afternoon toward the end of the first week, I shut down the machine and instructed the others to look for the guy's bottle, which I was sure he kept hidden somewhere around the viner. We found it tucked into a corner of the pea stack. As everyone watched, I dumped its contents on the ground, and then we all went back to work. In the days that followed, I expected the man to be hostile and difficult to work with, but he proved to not be a problem. He took his turn in the rotation from pitching peas to boxing peas to working on the stack. And we got the work done.

As viner boss, I earned $1.25 an hour; the crewmembers earned $1.00 an hour. We worked incredibly long hours, starting at dawn, around five thirty, and often staying at it until one or two the following morning. We could not leave the viner until the last pea was boxed and the machine cleaned for the next day's operation.

The summer I spent in the canning company warehouse, I learned what it meant to work long, hard hours—without complaining. The summer I worked as a viner boss was in many ways a short course in sociology. With long hours and hard work, viner crew workers sometimes had short tempers. I had to learn how to deal with each man's personality, his ups and downs. I learned the importance of treating each worker fairly so that no one felt he was working harder than another. Dealing with an alcoholic crewmember proved especially challenging, as I took a big risk in dumping the contents of his whisky bottle on the ground while he watched—and without knowing how he would react.

Those lessons learned on the job, in a real-life situation, proved invaluable. Years later, when I supervised people in vastly different situations, these basics still applied: treat people fairly and set an example for the behavior that you expect; when that behavior is violated, take action.

Cranberries

In October 1955, while I was waiting to report for army duty in January, I heard they were hiring workers at a cranberry marsh near Wisconsin Rapids. The pay offered was a dollar an hour. My brother Donald and neighbor boys David and Jim Kolka all enjoyed working outdoors and thought cranberry raking might be interesting work.

At that time, most cranberry harvesting was still done by hand (the shift to mechanical harvesting was just beginning). When we reported for duty, we each were given a pair of hip boots and a cranberry rake, which was a little wooden box with one open end with tines on it and two bow-shaped handles.

The cranberry bog had been flooded so that the ripe, red berries would float and thus could be more easily gathered. The water was around knee deep, and on chilly October mornings it was cold, cold, cold. We each pulled behind us a wooden bushel box tied to our belt with a short rope. When our rake was full, we dumped the cranberries into the box.

And when the bushel box was full, we carried it to the high ground that surrounded each bog, carefully navigating a narrow wooden plank placed across a water-filled ditch to get there. One misstep, and we would find ourselves in water up to our armpits. One inaccurate swing with the rake, and a tine would puncture a boot and we'd have a wet foot all day. My hip boots had patches upon patches by the end of the season.

The crew was made up mostly of young men, with a few middle-aged guys in the mix. We worked in a long line that stretched across the cranberry bog, about eight or ten of us, with the person on the far right setting the pace. We had to keep up with that person, and when our arms felt like they'd come out of their sockets, we considered drowning the guy. Some areas of the cranberry beds were weedy and difficult to rake, resulting in a lot of complaining and the whole process slowing down as our rakes got caught in the weeds.

After a week or so of cold, grueling work, several of us agreed that one dollar an hour wasn't enough. We decided to go on strike. Of course, we had no union and knew nothing about strikes except what we'd read about in the news, but it seemed like a good idea. So one afternoon, after a bit of discussion over lunch, all but one of us remained sitting at one o'clock, the official end of our break. The one fellow who went back to work said he wanted nothing to do with a strike—he was happy with the working conditions. But the rest of us were determined.

Looking at his watch, our foreman announced, "Time

to get back to work." We didn't move. He was flummoxed. "What's going on here?" he asked. "We've got lots of cranberries to rake."

"We're on strike," I said.

"You are what?" The foreman was in his fifties, a big, burly fellow and mean to the core. "You can't strike."

"But we are," Jim Kolka said.

Saying no more, the foreman jumped into his pickup truck and roared off. A half-hour later, he returned with the bog's owner, a pleasant-looking woman. She asked us why we were striking. We explained that for the work we were doing, we felt we should be getting more money. After a few minutes of discussion, she asked, "How about a compromise?"

"What do you suggest?" I asked, hopeful that she would suggest a five- or ten-cent increase in our hourly wage.

"I agree with you that this is not easy work, so I want to make it right with you all, because I've heard that you are hard workers."

We nodded our heads in agreement.

"Here's what I can offer," she said. "Each day, once you've reached a minimum number of bushels raked"—I've forgotten how many it was—"I'll give you an extra ten cents for each bushel you rake beyond that."

We agreed that that sounded like a reasonable compromise, and we went back to work, now keeping a record of each bushel raked. We worked harder than ever so we could capture that extra money. It was only later that I figured out how clever the owner had been. She not only made us feel good and praised us for our hard work, but she succeeded in making us work even harder. We finished raking her bogs a week earlier than usual—meaning we lost an entire week of wages because we finished sooner than expected.

I've often thought about the owner's approach to what could have turned into a much more serious confrontation. She probably could have easily replaced us, but she also knew that the harvest had to be completed before the snows and cold of November arrived, so keeping us engaged was important. She remained pleasant, agreed with us that the work was difficult, and indicated that she was willing to compromise. She made us believe that we were receiving a raise even as she encouraged us to work harder, and we ultimately received less pay.

Unfortunately, we weren't able to look far enough ahead to see that she would end up benefiting more than we would from our agreement. I learned to be careful what I ask for and to think it through to the end, as the results may not turn out as I hope. We would have been better off if we'd asked for nothing. It was a particularly hard lesson to swallow.

Ernie B.

Before he moved to our farm community, Ernie B. was a high school teacher in Chicago. After World War II, he felt like a lot of city folks who yearned for a "simpler life" in the country. Ernie decided to take up farming.

Ernie didn't look like a farmer—at least not to those of us who had grown up around farmers. He was short and skinny, and his thin arms had no hint of muscle. We all wondered why he moved to a farm to milk cows, cultivate corn, make hay, and earn a lot less money than he had in Chicago.

We soon discovered that our new neighbor was always trying something new. One of Ernie's innovations was a new way of storing green alfalfa hay. Anybody who knows a lick about making hay knows that you must allow it to dry before baling it. If you bale it while it's still green, it molds and rots, and no animal will eat it. And if you pack it too tightly in your barn, you'll burn down the barn with spontaneous combustion.

Ernie didn't store his bales of uncured hay in his barn. He dug a hole in the ground and packed it full with the bales.

When someone asked what he was doing, he said, "I'm creating a new generation of silage." In addition to having a head full of strange ideas, Ernie "talked city." Nobody in our neighborhood used words like *creating* or *generation* when they talked about silage or anything else.

Soon everyone in the neighborhood knew about the big hole at Ernie's farm full of uncured hay bales. But no one said anything. There was always an outside chance that what he was doing might indeed be a new way of making silage. We all knew how to make silage in our silos, but we—some us, anyway—were open to learning a new way, especially if it was easier.

A couple of months went by. Then Pa heard what had happened when Ernie took the cover off his underground silo. A powerful smell of rotten hay emerged and floated off across the road. Every last spear of alfalfa had rotted, and what was supposed to be an innovative silo had become an ordinary manure pile.

The news of this failure spread through the neighborhood about as fast as the news that the country schoolteacher had gotten in the family way. Once more, the farmers in our neighborhood were assured that "the old ways are the best ways" and went on making silage as they had always done it.

But Ernie wasn't discouraged. He had other ideas he wanted to try. At that time, grasshoppers were plentiful in our region, and the pests were devouring a substantial amount of the farmers' hay crop.

"I've got the answer to the grasshopper problem," Ernie told Pa when we ran into him at the gristmill one day.

"How so?" said Pa, remembering, of course, what happened with Ernie's recent silo project.

"Here's what I've done," Ernie said. "I fastened a piece of tin on the back of the sickle bar on my mower. Beneath the tin I fastened an old eaves trough."

"So how does it work?" Pa asked.

"You just pour some kerosene in the eaves trough——"

"Kerosene?" Pa said quietly.

"Yes, regular kerosene, the kind you put in lamps and lanterns. Then I drive the mower around the hayfield, cutting hay. When the sickle bar frightens a grasshopper, it strikes the piece of tin and is momentarily stunned. It falls into the kerosene and dies."

"That's it?" Pa said.

"Yes. I believe this invention will solve the grasshopper problem," said Ernie. "Stop by the farm on your way home, and I'll demonstrate how it works."

By the time we arrived at Ernie's farm, he had already hitched his team to the mower. We headed out to the alfalfa field, Pa carrying the kerosene can.

In the field, Ernie readied the mower for cutting and poured the eaves trough two-thirds full of kerosene. He said "giddap," and the team stepped off with the mower chattering behind. Ernie had a confident look on his face, a kind of "Like Thomas Edison, I've invented something important" look. I could see plenty of grasshoppers in the field, so the invention would easily be tested. Pa and I walked some distance behind the mower, watching grasshoppers hop over the metal piece and occasionally hit it and disappear from view. I figured they must have struck the metal, dropped into the kerosene, and died, like they were supposed to.

After cutting for a hundred yards or so, Ernie yelled "whoa," and the team stopped.

"How's it workin'?" asked Pa.

"Killed a grasshopper,"

"Just one?"

"Unfortunately, the rest escaped," Ernie reported.

"Why?" asked Pa.

"First bump I hit, the kerosene spilled. Have to do some more thinking about this invention. Something wrong with the mathematics."

I knew that Ernie had taught mathematics, but I didn't see what getting the numbers right had to do with spilling kerosene when you hit a bump. That seemed more like common sense than math. But I didn't say what I was thinking.

When several of the neighbors got together on Saturday night in back of Hotz's Hardware, the discussion quickly came around to Ernie and his new ideas. Pa shared the story of the grasshopper killer, and there was loud laughter. Of course, the new silo came up again. More laughter.

I believe it was Walter Bowen who put a stop to the fun-making. In all seriousness, Walter said, "One of these days Ernie will come up with something we'll wish one of us had thought of."

I've never forgotten Walter's words. It was people like Ernie B. who brought new ideas to our community, and even though they sometimes failed, they got us thinking. Maybe we should try something different, invent something new. In some ways, Ernie B. and people like him helped prepare us for the agricultural revolution that began after World War II.

Improvements

Pa often had ideas about how to make things easier on the farm, but he also knew that whatever he tried would be watched carefully by the neighbors. Because our family had lived in the neighborhood as long as or longer than most of the others, any kidding he drew for his new ideas was seldom said aloud, unlike the recently arrived "city farmers" who were openly mocked when they tried something new. So Pa often went ahead with new ideas without hesitation, once he had them figured out in his head.

In the days before mechanical barn cleaners, Pa was interested in devising a way to haul manure when the snow was too deep for the manure spreader to work. One day when he was in Wild Rose, he struck up a conversation with Jim Colligan at his welding shop. Colligan was handy with a welding torch and could make just about anything out of used parts and a good idea.

Pa had scratched out his idea on the back of an envelope and showed it to Colligan. After a long, careful look at Pa's crude drawing, Colligan said, "That just might work."

Back home, I helped Pa take apart the old bobsled that was stored behind the shed. It had two massive wooden runners with steel strips on their bottoms. Each was about six feet long, ten inches high, and three inches wide, and they were turned up at the front so they would glide through deep snow. We tossed the runners in the back of our 1941 Ford pickup and headed for Colligan's welding shop. "I've rustled up some other parts for a manure box," Colligan said when he saw the runners we'd delivered.

What Colligan did, following Pa's crude sketch, was to make what amounted to a manure-toting chariot on sleigh runners. It was high enough off the ground so when Pa pulled on a lever, the filled manure box would lift and allow its contents to slip to the ground—making a mini-manure pile out in the field. The chariot was designed to be pulled by our trusty team of horses. We all declared that it was quite the invention when Ross Caves, our local trucker, delivered it to our farm on a cold winter day.

Pa immediately wanted to try it out. The horses shied a little when he hitched them to the chariot, but soon Pa was standing way up in the chariot box with the team's harness lines in his hands. With a "giddy-up" they were off, Pa looking ever so much like a Roman gladiator riding in his bright green chariot as the team trotted around the yard. He was smiling from ear to ear.

The next day we pitched the chariot full of fresh cow manure, and Pa and the team were off to a far field. Unfortunately, there was no place for Pa to stand, except in the manure. But Pa had six-buckle rubber boots and didn't seem to mind this minor inconvenience. For several days all was well, the chariot performing as planned. But one day, after dumping the load of manure in the field, Pa spotted a jackrabbit in the fencerow. When he arrived back home, he asked me to fetch his 12-gauge double-barrel shotgun and a couple of shells. With the shotgun in hand, he trotted the team back out to the field.

A while later, I heard the shotgun's blast and figured Pa would be bringing home the rabbit. When he did finally appear, he was standing in the empty chariot and sawing on the lines of the team as it ran at a gallop, the chariot bouncing along behind them on the snow-packed road.

After we'd gotten the horses calmed down, I asked Pa what had happened. "Well," he said, "I spotted the jackrabbit under a little bush, held the lines between my legs, and fired the shotgun. When that gun went off, the team lit out a-runnin.' I fell down in the chariot but managed to keep hold of the lines. I drove them horses around the field three times before I dared drive them home. I don't know how many times I almost tipped over—this chariot ain't near as steady as it oughta be."

I couldn't stop laughing. Pa was covered with cow manure from the top of his wool cap to the bottom of his six-buckle books. When Jim Colligan heard about Pa's chariot adventure, he couldn't stop laughing, either. Not one farmer asked Colligan to build a manure chariot for them.

Pa and Jim Colligan came up with another idea, this one considerably more complicated than the manure-carrying chariot. During World War II, farm equipment manufacturers had turned to making war materiel and made almost no farm tractors. Restrictions also made it nearly impossible for farmers to buy the few tractors that were manufactured during that time; a farmer had to have a note from his county agricultural agent stating that the farmer needed a tractor in order to keep his farm production at a high level.

Pa was still doing all his farmwork with horses. So he asked Jim Colligan, "Could you make me a tractor?"

"You got an idea about how I might do it?" Colligan replied. He was always interested in trying something new.

"I was thinking we might start with an old truck, strip it down, and weld a drawbar to it."

Pa's idea wasn't nearly detailed enough for Jim to go on, but it was enough to whet the welder's appetite and get him thinking about how to convert an old truck into a farm tractor. A week or so later, Pa stopped by the welding shop and saw an old rusty truck.

"I found an old truck for you, Herm," Colligan said. "I think I can make a tractor out of it."

Colligan removed all the sheet metal down to the frame. Then he shortened the frame, leaving the engine and drivetrain in place. At the county shop in Wautoma, where the county's snowplows spent the summer, Colligan found some used snowplow tires, huge ones that he fastened on rims so that they would remain in place without putting any air in them. He fashioned some sheet metal over the engine and painted it with aluminum-colored paint.

Our new tractor had a truck's transmission, of course, meaning it had four speeds forward and one in reverse.

Only one speed, called dual-low, was suitable for farmwork. The other speeds were too fast; indeed, with the tall tires in back, any speed beyond dual-low was not only too fast, but dangerous.

One of the first things Pa did when he brought his new tractor home was to cut off the tongue on one of our wagons and fashion a hitch on the remaining section that could be attached to the tractor's drawbar. Now he could use his new tractor to pull a wagon, haul wood, maybe even haul oat bundles at threshing time or corn bundles at silo-filling time.

One of the most important uses Pa had in mind for his shiny new tractor was to pull a plow. But the only plow we had was a one-bottom plow that was pulled by a team of horses and required a sturdy man to hold its handles, especially in the stony ground our farm consisted of.

At the Sears store in Berlin, Pa saw just the plow for his new tractor. It was a David Bradley plow, the trade name for Sears, Roebuck farm machinery. The plow had two fourteen-inch plow bottoms and a special spring-loaded stone hitch, which meant that if the plow struck a stone too big to move, it unhitched from the tractor, thus avoiding breaking the plow points.

Plowing was one of the more difficult jobs for our farm team, especially when the possibility of striking a stone was near 100 percent. Pa's new plow and his homemade tractor worked well together and made the work easier for the horses. Even the most skeptical neighbors agreed on that. The part that didn't sit well with the neighbors was that the tractor required purchasing a different kind of plow than they now had, and they had to modify their wagons and other equipment by sawing off the tongues and attaching hitches. "What if the tractor doesn't work out and you ended up with a bunch of machinery that your horses can't pull?" they asked. "What will you do then?"

Although some people would always remain resistant to change, after the war new ideas and innovations flooded into farm communities, changing farm life from how it had been for generations. There was much for everyone to learn; driving a tractor bore almost no resemblance to driving a team of horses, nor did slipping a milking machine onto a cow instead of milking her by hand, or baling hay with a mechanical hay baler instead of pitching hay by hand onto a steel-wheeled hay wagon, or keeping food cold in a refrigerator instead of buying ice from the iceman. But as the old saying goes, "You ain't seen nothin' yet." Changes seemed to bombard our farm family at every turn.

As my mother and father confronted these changes and innovations, they considered each one carefully. Which of these new things could our family afford? Which would make life easier for us? How difficult would it be to use these new things, and in the case of innovations involving our farm animals, how would the animals adjust? My parents were not opposed to change, but they did not immediately buy every new thing that became available or try every new idea they heard about. They were deliberate and thoughtful—lessons I continue to put into practice, as change is a constant in all our lives.

Pennies

As change engulfed our neighborhood in the late 1940s, farm families had to choose which new methods and technologies to embrace and which to pass by. Many of the advancements were promoted by the local county agricultural agent and by the local banker, who was eager to provide loans to farmers who wanted to modernize their operation. Soon after the war, mechanical hay balers arrived and hay bales replaced loose hay. Farmers bought grain combines that not only cut the grain but threshed it as well. Grain binders and threshing machines became obsolete.

Forage harvesters appeared on many farms, replacing corn binders and silo fillers—and neighborhood silo-filling bees. Mechanical corn pickers replaced corn binders and shredders. Now farmers could fill their own grain bins, fill their own silos, and fill their own corncribs without the help of their neighbors.

Before and during the war, we saved some corn from our annual crop, drying the ears and using the shelled kernels for seed the next year. Before planting the corn crop, Pa would count out a number of corn seeds, shell them, roll them up in a wet sock, and place them in a quart jar. He put the jar in a sunny place for a week or so and then checked to see how many of the seeds had germinated. The best yield we could hope for in those days was about forty bushels of corn per acre. When hybrid corn varieties came on the market after the war, our corn yield doubled (some farmers who worked heavier, more productive soils might reach an unbelievable one hundred bushels per acre.) But there was a downside: hybrid corn cannot be saved for seed, so to achieve higher yields, farmers had to buy new seed corn each year.

My father did not purchase a grain combine, a corn picker, a hay baler, or a forage harvester. Instead, he hired a neighbor who owned the equipment to harvest our grain, pick our corn, and bale our hay. He did buy a tractor, and for a time he had half-ownership in a threshing machine. He bought a hammermill so he could grind his own cattle feed at home. He planted hybrid corn, but I don't recall that he ever sprayed any of his crops with weed killer. He believed in cultivating the soil, first with horses and later with a tractor; he said doing so not only killed weeds but also "gave the soil air."

He embraced artificial insemination, probably encouraged by the memory of the time we owned a vicious Holstein bull. It weighed over a ton and sought to destroy everything in its path, including Pa, me, and my brothers. We all breathed a sigh of relief when Ross Caves carefully loaded the animal onto his truck and headed for the stockyards in Milwaukee.

Through the county agricultural agent's office, Pa became a member of the Dairy Herd Improvement Association. Members of the program sent milk samples and a record of their cows' milk quantities to a lab; the lab sent back reports on the milk's butterfat content and the milk production of each cow. The DHIA proved to be a valuable tool in helping farmers determine which cows were performing well and which ones to consider culling from the herd.

But even as my father carefully chose which improvements to make on our farm, he remained ever frugal. The only loan he had was for the farm itself, and by the war's end he had paid off the mortgage and owned the farm outright. For a farmer, owning land was the ultimate possession. But many farmers who borrowed money found they couldn't make their payments on their loans and eventually lost their farms as a result.

Pa believe in the importance of learning from history, especially his own. As he often said, "If you don't know where you've been, you don't know where you're going." He felt there were many lessons to be remembered from what had happened to farmers during the Great Depression. After losing much of the money he had in the bank, he never trusted banks again. With farm prices so low, he watched every penny he spent, and he would never buy something unless he had saved the money to do it. "Don't live beyond your means" was one of his mantras.

Living within one's means is a rather simple idea, but I learned from watching those who did not grow up pinching every penny—as Pa described his frugality—just how devastating it could be. Losing a farm, losing a house, losing a way of life could all result from the simple idea of not living within one's means.

The Circle

Harry Chapin's song "The Circle" resonated with me from the first time I heard it. The simple phrase "All my life's a circle" from its chorus is filled with meaning for me. Chapin could have easily sung "All of farming's a circle," for it surely is. Each sunrise welcomes a new beginning; each sunset celebrates the work of the day completed. Each day brings the same chores in the morning, farmwork throughout the day, and chores in the evening. But each day is different as well, for some new joy, some new challenge, always appears.

On our small family farm, our days were a circle of repetition dictated by the seasons. The coming of spring marked the beginning of the farm's circle of activities. I remember well when the snow began melting one spring back in the 1940s. It had been a long, cold winter with many below-zero days and snow so deep the old-timers said they couldn't remember ever seeing such a tough one. But something was different that morning. Most obvious, the upstairs bedroom I shared with my twin brothers wasn't as cold as it had been on recent mornings. The thick frost that had covered the inside of the windows since November was melting, puddling on the windowsills. Rain splashed against the windows, one of the first sounds of spring. I looked out the window toward our snow-covered fields to the east and saw wisps of fog.

I pulled on my clothes, rushed downstairs, grabbed my barn lantern, and trotted to the barn for the morning milking. For the first time in weeks, the snow was mushy underfoot. The rich, subtle smell of spring was in the air. I noticed that the cows and calves were aware of the weather change as well. They were restless and eager to go outside, as they had been cooped up in the barn most of the time during the long winter months. After breakfast, we would let the cows outside to romp in the barnyard, to run with their tails in the air, to experience spring. To feel the rain on their backs and the soft snow underfoot.

Winter didn't give up easily. That evening, the rain changed to snow. But spring was waiting in the wings, for its chance to sneak in and push winter north for a few months. Even when I wondered if spring would ever come, of course it always did.

As the years passed, I came to enjoy the repetitions of each day and the expectations that came with each new season. And although the surprises that came our way nearly every day and every season were sometimes less than pleasant, they added spice and challenge to the circle. Now, as I think back to those days and their continual cycle of milking cows, cleaning barns, making hay, filling silo, threshing grain, and chopping wood, I've come to appreciate how spending the first sixteen years of my life embedded in the circle of farm life largely made me who I am today.

So many years later, I still look forward to and enjoy the seasonal changes. I do what my mother did, starting seeds in March, planting the garden in May, hoeing and weeding and harvesting in summer and early fall. In late winter, I study the seed catalogs in preparation for the garden season to come, just as she did.

Roshara, the central Wisconsin farm I have owned for more than fifty years, provides my family and me the opportunity to experience the circle of seasons as I did when I was a kid. After a long, quiet winter, spring arrives, sometimes coming in quickly, sometimes sputtering and a bit unsure of itself. It is followed by the heat and humidity of summer, with long days, balmy nights, and never-ending work in the garden. By September, a glorious fall sneaks up on us, reminding us that it is harvest time and treating us to an explosion of color across our acres of maple, birch, aspen, and oak. And then one day, usually in November, a cloudy sky gives up the first flakes of snow, and the circle rolls on.

I appreciate that my life is a circle. It is one of the most important things I learned from my growing-up years on the farm.

Final Thoughts

Today I understand how much I learned on our small family farm without realizing I was learning it. That early learning contributed greatly to who I am today.

I learned that people come in all sizes and shapes. Some are friendly, and some are not. Some believe as I do, many do not. Some go to church regularly and others not at all. I learned that it isn't easy to get along with all of them, but it is important to try. I learned to avoid making quick judgments about people based on how they look, how they dress, where they come from, their manner of speaking, who they voted for.

I learned that when my opinions differ from someone else's—often about politics or religion—I should step back and try to learn more about this person's position. I try to practice what I've always said to my students: "To know what you believe, you've also got to know what you *don't* believe." Occasionally I have learned from my mistakes what *not* to do and how *not* to act—this learning has been as important as its opposite.

As a young child, I learned the power of curiosity, to ask questions, to look where others did not choose to look, to listen to what others chose not to hear. I've never forgotten my father's admonition to always look in the shadows and listen for the whispers. I learned that time on the farm is different from that tracked by clocks and watches, that it has more to do sunrises and sunsets and the changing of the seasons.

I learned that numbers (especially numbers of dollars) do not always represent what is important—that the smell of freshly mown hay, the beauty of a sunset, and the power of a thunderstorm boiling up out of the west cannot be expressed in numbers. A number cannot describe the sheer beauty and mystery of a newborn, no matter if it's a new baby piglet, a newborn calf, or a new baby brother or sister.

I learned the importance of taking care of the land, treating it as a gift that was loaned to me as a farmer with the hope that I would respect it, care for it, and leave it in better shape than when it was given to me. I learned to follow the admonition of the Native Americans who see their responsibility for caring for the land so that seven generations in the future will benefit from their stewardship.

I learned to respect water. Growing up without indoor plumbing on a droughty, sandy farm where we never had enough water for our crops taught me the importance of working to keep water pure and in sufficient quantity so that all living creatures, not only those wishing to earn money from its use, can benefit. My father's instruction to "never curse the rain" has always remained with me.

I grew up surrounded by an assortment of animals—dairy cows, workhorses, hogs, chickens, barn cats, and an ever-present farm dog. I learned much from each of them. (Though I suspect I learned the least from the chickens.) I discovered that animals have their own personalities and that each animal wants you to know that and interact with it accordingly. Our farm dog, Fanny, provided an example of unconditional friendship to our entire family.

Of course, I learned the many skills that are part of farming and country life: how to use a shovel, pitchfork, hammer, and curry comb; how to teach a calf to drink out of a pail; how to milk a cow by hand and harness a horse; how to whittle a plug for the water jug with my jackknife; how to shock oats so the shock won't tip over; how to plow a furrow with a one-bottom plow and dig a pit for an outdoor toilet. But I also learned the 4-H pledge: *I pledge my head to clearer thinking, my heart to greater loyalty, my hands to larger service, and my health for better living for my community, my country and the world.* At my country school, I not only received a solid academic education, I learned how to stand in front of a group and "say my piece." And I learned the importance of everyone working together, sharing and caring for one another each day.

Perhaps most important, I learned to appreciate life's simple gifts:

- Silence
- Dark nights
- Never giving up hope

- Not fearing taking risks
- Friends
- Family
- A warm floor when I wake up on a winter morning and step out of bed

And I formed fundamental values that are still with me today:

- Live within your means and save money for the future.
- Appreciate what you have, even when you know others have more.
- Be optimistic. Tomorrow will be a better day; next year will be better yet.
- Work hard and do the best possible job, no matter what it is.
- Measure success by the extent that you help others.
- Realize that many things in life are more important than money.
- Understand the value of patience.
- Appreciate neighbors and be ready to help them at all times.
- Always be open to learning something new.
- Be honest.
- Show up on time—a little early if possible.
- Never boast. Allow your actions to show your worth.

- Think before you act.
- Don't talk until you have something to say.
- Maintain a sense of humor, even when times are tough.
- Remember that life is like a river. There are twists and turns, quiet spots and rapids, deep pools and shallow flats. But a river is always moving, always the same, yet always different.
- When we forget our histories, we forget who we are.
- Some things are best left alone.
- Remember to have fun.
- Appreciate the power of a nap.
- Never forget to take care of the land, for the land is the foundation of everything.
- Keep things simple.

Acknowledgments

For all of my writing, this work included, a huge thank you goes to my wife, Ruth, for her support and her practical, critical eye. "Will people understand what you are trying to say here?" She asks that question often.

Thank you to Kathy Borkowski, past director of the Wisconsin Historical Society Press, for her support of my work. Thank you to Kristin Gilpatrick, marketing manager, a never-tiring and brilliant marketer, who knows better than I how to put a "you'll want to buy this book" face on my work. And lastly, I can never say thank you often enough to Kate Thompson, Society Press director, who has worked with me on many books and has never failed in making each one better than I thought it could be.

About the Author

Photo by Steve Apps

Jerry Apps was born and raised on a central Wisconsin farm before electricity, indoor plumbing, and central heating came to the country. From first through eighth grade, he attended a one-room country school.

Jerry is a former county extension agent and professor emeritus at the University of Wisconsin–Madison, where he taught for thirty years. Today he works as a rural historian, creative writing instructor, and full-time writer and is the author of many fiction and nonfiction books on rural history, country life, and the environment. He has created five documentaries with Wisconsin Public Television, has won several awards for his writing, and won a regional Emmy Award for the TV documentary *A Farm Winter*. Jerry and his wife, Ruth, have three children, seven grandchildren, and two great-grandsons. They divide their time between their home in Madison and their farm, Roshara, in Waushara County.

Discover more books by Jerry Apps

Never Curse the Rain: A Farm Boy's Reflections on Water

Whispers and Shadows: A Naturalist's Memoir

The Quiet Season: Remembering Country Winters

Roshara Journal: Chronicling Four Seasons, Fifty Years, and 120 Acres

Living a Country Year: Wit and Wisdom from the Good Old Days

Every Farm Tells a Story: A Tale of Farm Family Values

Old Farm County Cookbook: Recipes, Menus, and Memories (with Susan Apps-Bodilly)

Old Farm: A History